A MAP FOR JOY:
Lessons From A Life Coach

Teri Johnson

Herttenberger Press
Kirkland, Washington

Herttenberger Press
12556 NE 120th Avenue
Suite 276
Kirkland, WA 98034

A Map for Joy: Lessons from a Life Coach
Copyright © 2004 by Teri Johnson
First edition printed June, 2004

ISBN 0-9755493-0-8
Library of Congress Control Number: 2004107720

Printed in the United States of America

Contents

Preface

Two years ago, I was nearing the end of certification for Legacy Leadership™, a leadership development program used within organizations. My colleagues and I were sitting at round tables of six when the facilitator, Jeanine Sandstrom, asked this question: "What is the legacy you want to leave the world?"

The answer erupted powerfully from deep in my chest and I could no more contain the words than we can contain a full river when it decides to expand. "I want to leave a map for joy!" I replied. Jeanine beamed at me and responded, "I believe you will, Teri." With her powerful question and the response that came from my spirit, the seed was planted. Since then, I have looked closely at the many clients, colleagues, friends and loved ones in my life who walk a more joyful path and distilled what I believe to be sixteen lessons that have the power to bring each of us more fully into greater states of joy.

These lessons build upon each other in a natural progression, with the first one laying an important foundation upon which all the others rest. I recommend that you read it first and then if you are inclined to skip around to whichever lesson might be most pertinent to you at the time, that foundation will support you.

With each lesson, there are exercises to take you further into your exploration. These are the kinds of inquiries you might make working with your personal coach. I suggest taking your time with these, as they can be powerful catalysts for greater awareness and growth. For example, after reading the first lesson, you might look at the exercises and choose one that appeals to you. Hold it in your mind for a week or so and see what emerges. A journal will be very useful to go along with the reading of this book, so that you may record your insights and "ahas" as you progress. With all that each of us experiences in a given week, it is easy to lose track of those nuggets of wisdom that could serve us so well if we remembered them. Sometimes, I'll write one of my discoveries on a three-inch Post-It note and choose a random future date in my calendar to remind me to revisit that principle. This is a great way to reinforce learning.

Each lesson is also sprinkled with relevant anecdotes and quotes. They come from clients, colleagues, friends and in the case of quotes, several historical figures and famous folks. These are included to link us more closely to one another. Here we are, having a human experience together and going through many of the same emotions, navigating similar challenges and having many of the same dreams and desires. It seems only fitting that we share our learning and well-earned wisdom to support each other in our growth.

Early in my experience of coaching clients, I began to see patterns repeated in person after person. It really brought home to me that we are so much more alike than different. Although the appearance and circumstances might be vastly different, what emerged to become this book were the universal truths that seemed to apply to each person, no matter what their background or position was.

I offer these lessons as a gift to my fellow travelers on the road of Life. May this map help you to create a journey that is more memorable, meaningful and positively *brimming* with joy.

Introduction

As I stand on the warm golden sand and look out at the vastness and power of the Pacific Ocean, I feel its waves shake the earth under me. I am filled with awe. Such beauty. What a perfect blend of delights to my senses, from the warm sand massaging my feet to the smell of the salty sea air to the red and purple streaks accompanying the sun on its nightly journey. There are golden sparkles scattered across the water, gulls playing on the breeze and the sound of laughter coming from up the beach. What a world we live in. My heart swells with joy as other pictures of inspiring beauty dance across my memory.

Imagine a Creator who designed all that we are now enjoying. In your mind's eye, picture solar systems, galaxies, planets and stars. Recall the beauty of a perfectly full, creamy white moon set against a velvet black sky. Then, remember the brilliance of the sun in a bright blue sky and how our world is decorated with myriad plants, animals and colors. Picture clear blue lakes, mountains and valleys. See the perfection of the design on each flower, and note that there is not one kind of red or blue flower, but hundreds of varieties, each delightful in its own right. This is a Creator who creates with exuberance, grandeur, grace and joy.

Joy, I believe, is our gift from Spirit. It's always there, ready to bubble up within us and erupt into laughter at any moment. We cover our natural joyfulness with fear, judgment, anger and a huge sense of responsibility. We sometimes forget that it is there and then, suddenly, like a ray of sun bursting through a cloud, it surprises us with its intensity in a moment when we need it most.

In my work as a life and business coach and teacher, I have noticed that many people seem to go on automatic pilot at some point in their lives and simply follow the path of least resistance. In following this well-worn, familiar path, they form habits in their way of thinking and being in the world, not stopping to challenge their assumptions. So, for instance, a person might form an opinion in their first job out of college that work is a drudgery to be endured and they may accept that and live that belief for twenty years or more.

According to what clients tell me, here is what usually happens: at some point, something painful gets their attention and they recognize a desire and willingness to create a change and seek out coaching. In working together, we identify what is really important to them, how they have or have not been honoring those values and we look at the assumptions that have driven their behavior and choices.

Almost always, they are thrilled to spend some time and energy in looking at and creating what they really want. So far, I haven't had a single client who didn't want to add more joy to the mix. Here's a little of what I have learned from them:

- We are more alike than any of us would have imagined

- No matter what our lives looked like yesterday, they can be transformed right now, today, by letting go of one limiting belief

- Allowing in more joy and wellbeing lights up all other areas of a life and brings about an astounding chain of events to support and sustain us

- We are amazingly wise, resourceful and capable with more access to deeper wisdom than we may be tapping

- Desire and willingness are the primary requirements for transformation

- Divine Spirit (or Universe or God, whatever you call that Life Force) supports us even when we don't know where we stand with that

- Joy is contagious. When you are laughing and playing and having a great time, people (and animals) are naturally attracted to you and will begin to laugh and enjoy themselves even if they don't know why you are laughing

The most powerful force in the Universe is love and this force brings joy with it. Sometimes, all that is required is to cease resisting and allow love to wash over us. Love for beauty, for generosity, for nature, for self, for others, for the Spirit that connects us all. We are naturally exuberant, playful and filled with happiness—just watch any two-year-old, kitten or puppy at play. Most of us begin to unlearn this at an early age and we can relearn it at any time.

My 20-something daughter told me recently that she remembers the day self-consciousness was born in her. It was her kindergarten year and her school had gathered in the auditorium for a concert being put on by the high school choir. She knew one of the songs and, inspired by their enthusiasm, she joined in the singing, rocking side to side in her chair, lost in the moment and fully enjoying the experience. Then, something odd happened. She felt the stare of many disapproving eyes, looked around and became self-conscious. She halted her singing and slumped back in her chair, puzzled about why she felt like she'd done something wrong.

Haven't we all allowed our joy to be squelched by disapproving eyes? Isn't it time we reclaim it and give each other the space to be outrageously happy whenever and wherever we're so blessed?

Although happiness is our natural state, many of us experience it much too infrequently. It can be cultivated. Clients, Spirit and Life have taught me what stands in the way and how to release it. That is why I wrote this book: to share a map for reaching a place of pure joy, as often as you like.

If you should experience any measure of delight while reading this book, or if a story unfolds as you incorporate these lessons, I'd love to hear about it. Send an email to: teri@intrepid-communications.com.

x

Understand the Power of Emotional Wellbeing

We Get What We Think About

We live in a Universe that is based on energy. Everything you see is made up of energy, including you and everyone else. If you looked at yourself through a powerful microscope, you would see molecules vibrating at a certain rate. If you watched closely, as your thoughts changed, the rate of vibration would change, too. Our thoughts determine our energy vibration. Since this is an attraction-based Universe, we get what we think about.

The more we are choosing thoughts that bring us to a joyful state, the more we attract other people, situations, events and things that bring us joy. There are some very compelling reasons why emotional wellbeing is the foundation upon which all the following lessons ride. The first is that everything we do, we do in order to feel good. Ultimately, every desire we have is for the *feeling* we'll get when that desire is met. We like to feel joyful and lighthearted, and when we do, we are in a place that allows us to attract more that will bring us those emotions.

Understanding this allows us to consciously choose thoughts that feel good in order to vibrate on purpose. We can see our emotions as a sophisticated guidance system that tells us when we are attracting what we want and when we are thinking thoughts that are driving those things away. We have much more control over the way we experience life than many of us might believe. Finding our joy not only feels good in the moment, it brings about more to be happy about. Understanding the power of emotional wellbeing is like unlocking a magic door that leads to the kind of life we only thought possible in the movies.

You are the Creator, Director of your Movie

You are the creator of the movie that is your life. You cast the characters, design the set and backdrop, choose your costume, and decide what the story is about. What is your life story about? Whatever you have written up to now is not as relevant as what you'll write today. The greatest power you wield is in your right now. What happens in this chapter? What strengths does the hero/heroine (you) now have to build upon? What will you break free from? What will you leave behind, having learned the lesson?

> *"Here, then is a practical key to receiving more of what you want in your life: Become one with what you want. If you want to receive more joy in your life, become one with the joy all around you."*
> — **Laurence G. Boldt,** ***The Tao of Abundance***

We are immensely creative and powerful beings, born to be the authors of our own lives. We are free to choose what our story will be about. We can write anything we want on the blank page that is each day. What an amazing gift we have in getting a new beginning in every day! We can decide to bring in laughter, joy, exuberance and connection. We can decide to design environments that support our creative natures. We can decide what kind of work would give us the greatest measure of satisfaction and pleasure. We can decide what kind of relationships would bring us a sense of delight. We can decide to move through the world at a pace that is delicious for us. We can *decide* to be a positive, joyful light in the world.

> *"I define joy as a sustained sense of wellbeing and internal peace - a connection to what matters."*
> — **Oprah Winfrey**

As we get clearer and clearer about what we want, unfolding new arenas will open before us. All our natural strengths can be utilized to support our learning and play.

Because you have picked up this book, it is apparent that a sense of joy is important to you. Great! You have just placed yourself at the launching point for more to appear, because the starting place was the decision that you want it. You have been heard and will be accompanied by Spirit on this journey. Pay attention to what moves you, what gives you goosebumps. Those are clues about what is true at a soul level for you.

> *"I cannot believe that the inscrutable universe turns*
> *on an axis of suffering; surely the strange beauty of*
> *the world must somewhere rest on pure joy!"*
> **— Louise Bogan**

Emotional Wellbeing is Your Number One Priority

When I suggest that emotional wellbeing is their number one priority some clients begin to wiggle and squirm in their chairs, especially the women. That's because we have been taught to put ourselves last. For many, there is no more noble deed than to die giving their last breath of energy serving someone else. And then what? If you give all of you away until there is nothing remaining, your family and friends are deprived of the unique experience of you. And who knows what *you* might be missing.

In order for you to give from a place of joy and abundance to others, you must create and maintain that for yourself. Your emotional wellbeing is the place from which all generosity flows. That wellspring is where you find strength for big challenges and compassion for yourself and others. It is where patience, tolerance and yes, even love is born. Mustering the capacity to love others when you are in pain or out of balance is difficult, at best. So, how do you create a sense of joyful wellbeing?

Increasing Awareness

The first step in moving toward a more joyful experience of life is to turn up your awareness. Upon awakening, what is your emotional state? Do you awake enthused, excited to begin your day? Are you starting out the day on a high or low note? Are you aware that you are in the driver's seat of your mind and you can direct your thoughts to whatever gives you peace, balance and calm?

 My client, Susan* found that she rarely awakened in an "up" state of mind, and so the start to her day was kind of sluggish. She didn't mind getting up, but she hated getting up and moving immediately, while she was still sleepy. Together, we designed a short morning ritual that allowed her to ease into the day. She chose a few motivational tapes that she could listen to while enjoying a hot cup of coffee in bed first thing after awakening. In twenty minutes, she found herself more clearly focused and excited about the day. Her energy was stronger and she was more motivated to get going than she ever had been. This ritual is now a favorite part of her day.

●　　　●　　　●

Begin to notice your thoughts and which ones bring you wellbeing and which ones bring you down. You many become aware of some familiar voices in your head, like:

- The voice of fear: "Why is she so late? Something awful must have happened. Oh my GOD, what has happened? What will I do?"

- The voice of doubt: "What was I thinking? I can't possibly handle a project of this scope. I'm going to look like an idiot."

- The voice of scarcity: "I shouldn't tell her about my sales strategies; she might move past me and get that promotion I've been working so hard for."

*Indicates a name change to protect the privacy of clients.

As you notice the pattern of these voices over the next week, begin to direct your thoughts to what gives you happiness, turning away from draining thoughts as soon as you notice them.

Pay attention to what you say aloud, too. Listen with your inner ear to the conversations you're having with your family members, friends and colleagues. What is the pattern there? What do you find yourself talking about most of the time? What are the stories you are likely to repeat to different people? In your conversations, where do you dwell most, in the past, present or future? There is only one place we can make a difference and change things: in the current moment.

Whether we realize it or not, we often replay unhappy times over and over again by repeating them to anyone who will listen. This only adds energy to that situation and increases the likelihood that we will draw that experience to us again.

"Your own words are the bricks and mortar of the dreams you want to realize. Your words are the greatest power you have. The words you choose and use establish the life you experience."

— **Sonia Choquette**

Remember that we are composed of energy and are constantly vibrating. Our vibrations change with thoughts and words spoken. As we vibrate, we attract. If we vibrate with pleasant thoughts we attract more that pleases us. If we vibrate with angry thoughts, we attract more that angers us.

In the chapters ahead, we will examine these and other patterns and step by step, you will begin to create your personal map for joy. For now, you are gathering information. Look around you. What are your surroundings like? Are they orderly and calm or chaotic and cluttered? What kinds of surroundings give you the most satisfaction? Where do you feel peaceful? What colors are you naturally drawn to? Whose home do you enjoy visiting most and why?

Begin to notice the kinds of places where you experience a sense of belonging, aliveness and joy.

 I loved going to my parents' house for a long weekend. They had a big, sprawling rock house on the shores of a lake. Up the hill was an aunt's house that we slept in during our visits. We had the comaraderie of family and friends, plenty of food and drink and the beauty of the woods and lake. At night, we walked up the hill to a private, quiet, tidy place to sleep, to awaken at our own pace and savor a cup of coffee while watching the sunrise. Later, we'd join the rest of my family in the noise and laughter of my parents' home. For me it was a delicious blend of togetherness and solitude and quite a joyful experience.

● ● ●

As you are finetuning your awareness, notice the people who you enjoy being around. Do you feel energized by them? And who are the people you feel drained by?

Exercise

Think back over the last year and list 10 times or events when you remember feeling happy:

1.

2.

3.

4.

5.

6.

7.

8.

9.

10.

What do you notice?

What are the common elements?

How can you incorporate more of these in your life today?

◆   ◆   ◆

Breaking Free — Making the Necessary Changes

Once you begin to notice the elements that allow access to a greater sense of wellbeing, you can design your life to include them in just the right amounts. There is no one-size-fits-all here. For instance, each of us requires a certain amount of interaction and a certain amount of solitude for maximum happiness. It's up to you to decide what the right measure is for you in these and other areas, like:

Physical activity	Music	Friends
Spiritual Connection	Travel	Entertaining
Career Challenge	Adventure	Sex
Reading	Movies	Learning
Relaxing	Meditating	Family Time
Self Reflection	Helping Others	Sleep

 Marta* found herself growing further and further apart from her husband of many years. They had two wonderful sons together, so she stayed in the marriage, trying to make it work. Eventually, the distance between them became palpable and she was terribly unhappy. The rest of the family wasn't thriving, either. "It got to the place where I just couldn't be myself in my own home without being ridiculed. Our beliefs were vastly different and we just couldn't reconcile that. Every conversation would lead to a disagreement. Leaving was a tough choice to make, but immediately all four of us felt the relief of tension."

Marta moved to an apartment not far from the boys and their dad. She began building a life that is making her happy. She started a new job and is making friends with people she truly enjoys being around. She is close enough that her sons come by for dinner several times a week. For the first time in her life, she is putting her own needs first and says she's feeling more optimistic than she has in a long time. Her home is now often filled with the sounds of heartfelt conversations, laughter and joy. Her sons are experiencing harmony in both their homes.

●   ●   ●

It takes courage to make big changes in our lives, and yet when we stand up for ourselves, everybody wins. Each of us deserves happiness. It is our responsibility to create it. When you learn how to direct yourself to a constant state of wellbeing, you can quite literally change your entire experience of life. By making this your *number one* priority, you give yourself the wonderful gift of your own attention, and as much as anyone else, you are worthy of it.

When you find yourself feeling out of balance, stop and find a quiet moment to reflect on what is missing or feels out of whack for you. Then take whatever action steps are required to return you to a centered, peaceful state. Slow, deep breaths can be of immense help here, and sometimes a simple change of perspective about something is just what is required. Give yourself permission to pause and identify whatever it is that you want or need, and proceed from there.

> *"Your life can be as wonderful or as horrible as you*
> *allow it to be. It all depends upon the thoughts that*
> *you practice. And therein lies the basis of anyone's*
> *success: How much do I practice thoughts that*
> *bring me joy, and how much do I practice thoughts*
> *that bring me pain?"*
>
> —Abraham

When conducting career-transition workshops, I share this philosophy with attendants. Sometimes they see it as impractical, until we discuss the ramifications of being out of emotional balance. For instance, many professionals are coming from a very fearful emotional state when they have been laid off. They are looking at the big "what ifs" and scaring themselves. When they are in that frame of mind, they launch into the job search immediately, without giving themselves time to heal, to think about what they've learned and what they really want next. Then, they push themselves relentlessly, often spending 40 to 50 hours a week looking at the Internet, at ads, attending job fairs and calling on people. After a few weeks of that they are confused, exhausted and discouraged. In addition, they have adopted the attitude of desperation, which colors all they see. When they do get an interview, they are tired, out of balance and do not have access to their best thinking because of the emotional fog they've created.

By contrast, a person who is committed to his or her wellbeing would enjoy some time off and reflect on what they really want. They might call on their Higher Power, whatever they hold that to be, for guidance and assistance. Perhaps they would work with a career coach or counselor to help them come up with a plan that fits their style. They would take excellent care of themselves, knowing that self-care is an important investment in their future. They would take relaxation and leisure breaks between job searching activities to keep a sense of balance. Then, when a good opportunity was presented, they would have access to their own clarity and be able to show their value in an interview situation. When they do accept an offer they will begin it feeling strong and refreshed from the recent break rather than exhausted from a panic-driven search.

Is there any life situation or challenge that would not be enhanced by a strong sense of wellbeing? I don't think so. My experience working with people tells me that we simply are not taught how important it is and how to cultivate it because our society in general is reacting to fear most of the time. If a person reads the daily paper in their city and watches a television news program, they are exposed to hundreds of fearful and negative messages. How many of those messages are important to you personally? It's more than we need to take in every day. We are overloaded with fearful messages and there is no kind of balance with stories of the wonderful things that are happening in our world because *bad news sells*. Take a break from the news and read a novel instead, or listen to some favorite music. Design your day in ways that support your sense of happiness. You have the right to choose what you let in and you are the only one who can exercise that choice. Changing these kinds of life-long habits can be a challenge, and you are worth it.

 One emotional stresser for me personally is too much incoming noise. I'm very aware of all the sounds in an environment. For instance, if I'm in a crowded restaurant, I hear the conversations at my table and all the nearby tables, I hear the music, I hear the noise of dishes clinking in the kitchen and if there is traffic noise outdoors, I hear that, too. Combine that with trying to have a meaningful conversation with the person across from me and my noise filter goes on overload. I feel stressed.

So, how do I create meaningful group dinners while honoring my emotional health? My first choice is to have dinner parties at home, where the music is consciously chosen to complement conversation, not compete with it. I have no more than eight guests at a time so everyone has a chance to talk with the others and the noise is not overwhelming. Another option is to choose restaurants that create a quiet, intimate atmosphere. They are sometimes a little more expensive than a national chain, because they aren't rushing people through to get volume, and the trade-off is fine with me. My friends in the restaurant industry say that the music and acoustics (no carpet) are carefully chosen to keep traffic moving, which improves their bottom line. We can choose to be as selective to improve our wellbeing and pleasure.

•   •   •

Know that as you begin to honor yourself more deeply, those around you will notice and may react with questions, comments, or criticisms. You have an opportunity then to let them know what you are doing and why, and in this way you are setting a healthy example of very good self-care.

 For Reflection

1. Looking back over the day, where is your energy drained?

2. What daily rituals would you like to let go of?

3. What are some ways you can improve the quality of your day?

4. What would be a delightful addition or subtraction?

When we are in a state of emotional wellbeing, we are calm, relaxed and open to possibility. We breathe deeply and have the capacity to laugh easily and move with fluid grace. We are flexible and playful and willing to experiment. We enjoy life and look forward to more good times.

Imagine watching two dancers. One is loving the dance: she

spins, she twirls and leaps with enthusiasm, smiling all the while. Her pleasure and joy are self evident and contagious; the energy of happiness fills the audience and we soar with her, caught up in her sense of freedom and exuberance. Now picture another dancer. He is self conscious and rigid. He moves with caution and clearly isn't having much fun. It is almost painful for us to watch as he suffers through the number, focused on his fear and certainty that he is going to mess up. We all breathe a sigh of relief when it is over.

Life *is* a beautiful, magical dance. As we each take to the dance floor, my desire is for us to dance with a sense of pure joy and abandon, completely unselfconscious and savoring every delightful movement.

Love and Accept Yourself Unconditionally

All is well. Truly it is.

We come into the world knowing that we are perfect and all is well in the Universe. As we begin to assimilate and others exert their well-intended influence on us, our confidence flags and we begin to feel fear and shyness. As children, we hear the adults in our lives ridicule those who are different in some way. We begin to believe that there is a very narrow and specific set of rules and standards we must abide by to be loved and accepted even by our own families. Then, when we compare ourselves to others and decide we don't measure up in some way, the disappointment and anger is turned inward where it shrivels happiness and dissolves self worth.

It is time to stop judging ourselves and others so harshly. Finding fault with every person, every situation and every element of life has become a habit. This critical view of self, life and others is a path that leads directly away from joy. We are each a unique, Divine, beautiful expression of All-there-is. No two of us is exactly alike, and yet we are One. How different our experience of life might be if we were taught from the beginning to love ourselves and others unconditionally. *Unconditionally*. Think about what that really means. For me, it means no matter what mistakes we make, regardless of how cranky we are, no matter how poor our choice of words or actions, we are still treasured, loved and valued.

"Be in love with the contrast that produces desire."
—**Abraham**

Wouldn't it be grand if someone had told us, "You are perfect and they are perfect and isn't the contrast delightful?" Instead, we are frequently shown from a very early age that "different" equals bad.

Imagine a mother saying to her toddler, "Yes, Tommy, we do come in different colors and shapes and sizes; isn't it wonderful? Your friend, Alice has chocolate-brown skin. Isn't it beautiful? Look how her smile shines!" Or a father, saying to his teenaged daughter, "I love the way you express yourself so freely with your colorful clothes and vibrant music... I'm learning so much through you."

Embrace Magnificence

If we could fully embrace, without a doubt, the idea that we are truly magnificent beings, then any choices that didn't reflect that belief would be seen with full confidence that we will all figure it out. We would say, for instance, "Oops, I got a little off track back there, but now I see that and I'm getting right back on," or "Wow, Susan is not her usual cheery self today. I know what a lovely person she is, so she must be grappling with some challenge. She will work it out and I am sending her an extra measure of light today."

"I find that when we really love and accept and approve of ourselves exactly as we are, then everything in life works."
—**Louise Hay**

Most of us have pure intentions that are very straightforward:

- We want to love and be loved
- We want to experience freedom and joy
- We want to interact with others in a way that's stimulating and fun
- We want to explore and discover
- We want to make a contribution

- We want to have a place of beauty, comfort and rest to return to between adventures

You Have a Sophisticated Inner Guidance System: Your Emotions

It is when we perceive that any of those is threatened that we start to think about what we don't want and then begin to align with that vibration and feel bad. In our interactions with ourselves and others we have a very reliable way of knowing when we are off our natural path: When we don't have a sense of wellbeing. The discordant emotions can be thought of as an accurate indicator to show us where we departed from our true selves. For example, have you had the experience of being in a group, then one person leaves and the others point out that person's shortcoming and you feel sort of uncomfortable? But then you offer some juicy information that adds fuel to the fire....and suddenly you don't feel so good. You feel a little nausea, so you leave, replaying the conversation in your head as you drive home. You wonder what they might have said about you. By the time you get home you just want to lie down, because you are suddenly very tired.

In that scenario, each time you made a choice that was not in harmony with who you really are (magnificent!) your emotional and physical guidance system let you know.

David* is talented in many areas and well respected in his industry. When he began the exercise of noticing his internal dialog, he was shocked at how harsh the criticisms were. The first time he noticed that derogatory voice was when he had accidentally broken a favorite wine glass. "Clumsy idiot! You should be more careful," he heard his inner critic say. After that, he began noticing a continued running commentary in his thoughts. It sounded a lot like an immature, petulant bully, and once he was aware of what was happening, he took stock of how draining those criticisms were and decided to change the behavior. Giving himself encouraging statements felt kind of silly at first, but over the course of a few weeks, he noticed that he didn't feel like he had to hurry all the time. He was much more relaxed and confident that whatever challenge he undertook, he would do well. David was surprised at what a toll the inner critic was exacting on his wellbeing and relieved to find a way to reverse the pattern.

●　　　●　　　●

"The greatest discovery of my generation is that a human being can alter his life by altering his attitudes of mind."
— **William James**

Exercise

Spend about five minutes looking at yourself in the mirror, with the deliberate intention of seeing yourself with loving, compassionate eyes. See yourself the way you would see a treasured, dear friend. Allow love to emerge for you and all you have experienced in this life…all you are trying to be, do and have. Place your palms on either side of your face and hold it tenderly in your hands the way you would hold someone you treasure. Allow whatever emotions you feel to emerge and be expressed. How does this feel? Are you nourished by your own acknowledgment? Begin to find ways to extend love and appreciation to *you*, because you are quite deserving of it and no one else knows how much.

◆　　　◆　　　◆

Are you familiar with the voice in your head that makes a running commentary about everything you do? Some people call it The Critic, the Gremlin or the voice of your ego. The point is that whatever you call that voice, it is part of you. For most of us, it is unreasonably demanding, critical and sometimes even belittling and mean.

Imagine how different your experience of life would be if you treated yourself like you would treat a young person you were mentoring. What if your inner voice gave you words of encouragement and acknowledged your effort and progress?

We will spend our entire lives listening to this voice. Begin now to transform it into a nurturing, supportive partner that you can count on to encourage and uplift you in every situation. Every success recipe calls for a good measure of self-confidence. It is nearly impossible to develop a high regard for ourselves if we are continually criticized and harshly judged.

"Our lives always express the result of our dominant thoughts."
— **Soren Kierkegard**

Every Relationship We Have with Others is a Mirror of the One We Have with Ourselves

When we begin to create the space of unconditional love and acceptance for ourselves, amazing things happen. It is from this place that joy is born. We have more capacity to be loving and forgiving of others. Unconditional regard for ourselves gives us many things, including:

- The freedom to make mistakes
- The ability to simply notice without judgment
- The freedom to be ourselves and know that we are enough
- Nurturing
- Encouragement
- Support for ideas

Here is some of what unconditional self-regard takes away:

- Fear of failure or making a mistake

- The pressure to meet other people's expectations
- Concern over measuring up
- Self-criticism and flagellation
- The need to make others look small
- The need to prove anything

This is heady stuff. Having an advocate look out for our own comfort, wellbeing and joy is a powerful shift for most of us who were taught to put ourselves last. It may seem odd at first. Allow yourself to give it a try, one small step at a time. Start out with one day of giving yourself the gift of unconditional love and acceptance. As you move into that day in the morning, think about all you have accomplished. Then, set your intentions for each segment of the day, deciding what you want to experience as you move from project to project. Stop every hour or so and listen for some uplifting thoughts, like, "I have plenty of time to do everything I've planned today, so let's relax and get comfortable in this work I'm doing now." At the end of that day, look back at how different it was. What do you notice?

Were there places where you fell into old critical habits? What prompted that? How would you do it differently next time? Are you willing to be accepting of your beginning status at this new thought process?

There are many ways you can begin to incorporate this into your way of being. Perhaps you start with a place that is particularly vulnerable to self criticism, and commit to being more accepting of yourself in that one area. A personal example: for me, that area might be disorganized workspace. For today, I will be kind and accepting of myself around that issue and think of new ways to support growth and change there. Maybe I could give myself an extra five minutes after each client call to put away all notes and files related to that client, take time for a glass of water and clear up my space a little. Part of what would support me in that is not to answer every incoming call myself during that time. I could let voice mail or my assistant take messages to free me up during this part of my day and return calls in the afternoon when my energy takes a dip anyway. Wow! That supports me to make significant changes in the flow of my day. Imagine what a ripple effect there might be when I apply this principle to other areas. Although we have the freedom to design our lives in ways that totally support us, we rarely think of it because we are conditioned to go along with the program everyone else is on. It takes confidence and belief in yourself to say, "I think I'll design my own program."

A point of clarification here: it is assumed there is an understanding that your intention is to be the best you can in all areas. I am not suggesting unconditional self-love and acceptance as a way to absolve you of all responsibility for your actions. Indeed, we are each responsible for all of our choices. If you exhibit behaviors that are harmful or unkind to yourself or others, seek professional assistance to support new learning and protect those in your life from harm. When you know you're doing all you can to move forward in your development it is much easier to love and accept all of who you are.

> *"A strong positive mental attitude will create more miracles than any wonder drug."*
> — **Patricia Neal**

Beware the Pleaser

We are adaptable people—we have had to be in order to survive. Adaptability and flexibility are good in the right measure. Yet, if you find yourself continually bending and adapting to meet other people's expectations, you may be shortchanging yourself. Each of us has natural preferences about many things: when to awaken; when, how much and what to eat; how to arrange our days; how much people contact, radio or television to allow in, etc. If you are a pleaser, you many override your natural preferences to accommodate a spouse or others. You might even be convinced that there is something wrong with being a night owl when most of the world operates on a 9-to-5 schedule. When you override too many of your natural preferences, it's like trying to swim against the current. Accept your own nature and preferences and honor them as much as you can and you will begin to be carried along by them rather than swimming upstream.

"To know what you prefer instead of humbly saying Amen to what the world tells you you ought to prefer, is to have kept your soul alive."

— **Robert Louis Stevenson**

 Jana* is an artist who works from a home studio. Her husband was recently laid off from a high tech position and she found herself making adjustments to keep pace with him. She stayed in bed longer in the mornings because he wanted to enjoy sleeping in. Therefore, she started working about two hours later than her normal routine, which meant that either she lost two hours of productivity or worked later into the evening, altering their family dinner schedule and relaxation time.

After a few weeks, Jana noticed an irritability that was just under the surface most of the time. She had also adjusted her pace to her husband's slower pace and found herself restless and anxious because she wasn't using enough of her naturally high energy to get tired at night, which was affecting her sleep. Finally, she took a close look at where all the anxiety and stress was coming from and shared her discoveries with her husband. He completely understood, since he had felt out of step with her faster pace and high energy for years. They decided it was better for each of them to honor their own natural rhythms, and designed a schedule that accomplished that and gave them together time as well.

● ● ●

The Perfectionist

Many of the clients I work with are high level executives or business owners, and wear a variety of hats not only in a professional capacity, but at home, too. When they demand perfection in all their performing roles, burnout isn't far behind. There isn't a lot of room for joy when a person is in that space. Many of us have an unrealistic idea of how much and how well we "should" be producing. "Should" according to whom? Expecting or demanding that we put the same level of intensity toward every task we attempt in a day is unreasonable. We must ask ourselves, "What's important to me now?" often enough that we become adept at dropping the lower priority items off our list, delegating, or letting "good enough" be good enough. Does it really matter that your child's bed has lumps and wrinkles in it when he's made it? You know you are a perfectionist if you see yourself in this description: you wince at the bed and remake it or enter into an argument with your child about how a job worth doing is worth doing right. Then, you chide yourself later for not being a better (perfect) parent. Give yourself and everyone else a loving, wide margin for error.

 My dear friend, Phyllis, recently shared with me that she had been going through family photos to divide among her children, who were beginning to decorate homes of their own. As she looked at herself as a young bride, she felt a wave of compassion and surprise. She remembered feeling self conscious in her bridal gown, certain that she wasn't thin enough. As a mother of four looking backward in time, she realized that she really did look lovely and her weight was just fine. She was saddened at how hard she'd been on herself and realized she missed out on feeling beautiful on her wedding day over a couple of pounds that, in her young eyes, made her seem less than perfect. "I'm not going to do that again. Whatever weight I am, I am. It's not going to rob me of any more happiness."

●   ●   ●

When you see yourself through compassionate eyes, being as loving, encouraging and supportive of who you are as you would be with a beloved friend, it changes the nature of your relationship to you. The critic or taskmaster is gone, replaced by a caring, thoughtful voice of encouragement.

This allows you to stop judging and measuring every decision, every action, and trust yourself to do your best. You begin to "fill the well" with all you need to be whole, strong and happy. You then have a place of abundance from which to share. You will begin to be more patient and kind with others, which can dramatically improve your relationships. You become a blessing to yourself and everyone around you.

> *"True acceptance comes when you can embrace and appreciate your body as it is right now, and no longer feel that you need to alter it to be worthy of someone's love—most especially your own."*
> — **Cherie Carter-Scott, in *If Life is a Game, These are the Rules***

 For Reflection

1. How often do you stop to acknowledge yourself for something you have achieved?

2. What would self-acknowledgement and gratitude look like to you?

3. Do you celebrate your accomplishments? What kinds of celebrations give you the greatest sense of pleasure?

4. Where are the places the harshest critic shows up in your life?

5. Are there particular events or times of year that trigger closer self-recrimination? How might you set up reminders to increase awareness and support for yourself at these times?

6. If you find the voice in your head uttering harsh criticism in the next day or two, how could you rewrite the script using what you've learned here?

7. How can you best teach the young people in your life to be kind to themselves?

Hold No Grievances

Move Through Life With the Grace of a Light Heart

A joyful person is one who is able to experience fully the magic of right now, this moment. They don't wallow in past disappointments and they don't worry about the future. They are grounded in the present with a sense of trust about past, present and future; they know all is well.

How is this done? By travelling lightly. In the group work I do, we always begin the discussion with a guided visualization, where we hand over all our concerns to a strong spirit, who will easily carry them for us so that we are free to be fully present for the time we are together. The invitation is that at the end of the evening, if they choose to take those burdens back from the strong spirit, they can. No one ever does. Why would they? Releasing all that old baggage and being free to explore with each other feels wonderful.

> *"Finish each day and be done with it. You have done what you could. Some blunders and absurdities no doubt crept in; forget them as soon as you can. Tomorrow is a new day; begin it well and serenely and with too high a spirit to be encumbered with your old nonsense."*
>
> **— Ralph Waldo Emerson**

Most of us accumulate grievances every day. The cat throws up yet again on a prized rug. Our child leaves a trail of pajamas and rejected attire from the bathroom to the kitchen. We get into the car our teenager used last night only to realize it is out of gas. By the time we navigate traffic, put in a full day at work and prepare dinner, chances are we have registered dozens of irritants throughout the day. Add to that the BIG grievances we hold for when our pride is hurt or someone we love tramples our feelings. We simply cannot contain all these without poisoning our emotional, physical and spiritual systems. Negative emotions like anger, fear and resentment are toxic to our health and happiness. They create stress. Experiencing joy is difficult when we are angry, resentful and stressed out.

> *"The key to learning the lesson of compassion is realizing that you are in control of the erection or destruction of those barriers that create distance between you and others. You can choose to dissolve those barriers when you want to connect with the heart of another human being."*
>
> — **Cherie Carter-Scott**, in *If Life is a Game, These are the Rules*

Exercise

To see how much "stuff" you are holding onto, answer the following questions quickly, without a lot of thought:

- Who am I mildly irritated with?

- What situation do I play over and over in my mind?

- If I could hand over all the grievances I'm currently holding, what would be on that list? (*Write until you are complete.*)

◆   ◆   ◆

"The weak can never forgive. Forgiveness is the attribute of the strong."

— Mahatma Gandhi

How do we begin to let go of all grievances? We begin with ourselves. All of us have made choices that didn't turn out the way we'd hoped. With hindsight, it is so easy to say, "Duh, that was an obvious mistake." Let it be okay that your life is an experimental process. Allow yourself the freedom to move forward a step at a time, knowing that there will be missteps and fall downs. Build room in for those, and maybe even allow laughter for those moments. Have you ever held the fingers of a toddler as she learned to walk? Treat yourself with the same encouragement and compassion and celebration you would give her, for you are often doing something for the first time and expecting to do it perfectly. Who needs that kind of pressure—at any age?

Let go of any hard feelings you might be harboring against yourself for poor choices. Recognize that everyone else makes poor choices at times, too. Release them from any guilt you would send their way. Our choices can affect everyone around us, and when we make errors others sometimes feel the sting, and vice versa. Let it be all right that we are all learning at the same time, and may occasionally step on each others' toes.

Forgive yourself for any unkind words or acts. Don't play them over and over in your head; that does nothing but make you feel guilty and guilt serves no useful purpose. In fact, guilt often leads you to attack someone else in an attempt to escape from the weight of it.

As soon as you make a mistake that affects someone else, simply apologize, forgive yourself and move on. If there are choices from your past that haunt you, they are robbing you of a measure of happiness today and doing nothing for the other person.

> *"Anger makes you smaller, while forgiveness forces you to grow beyond what you were."*
>
> **— Cherie Carter-Scott**

Remember that you may be shifting some life-long patterns, habits and beliefs. That may stir up strong emotion. It will take time to release those patterns of behavior that don't work and create new ones that do. The result you get will be worth it, so be patient with yourself in implementing these ideas. Feel free to edit. Use the ones that work, tweak the ones that don't exactly fit until they work for you. Discard whatever isn't in congruence with your authentic self.

Sometimes a ceremony helps you fully release an old wound. Use the forms provided here. Alter them to suit you or create your own. Complete one for every perceived offense that you revisit. Then design a ceremony or ritual of release. Burn them, shred them or tear them up. Whatever you do, let them go.

> *"It really doesn't matter if the person who hurt you deserves to be forgiven. Forgiveness is a gift you give yourself. You have things to do and you want to move on."*
>
> **— Real Live Preacher**

Exercise  A Ritual for Healing

1. Choose a time when you will have about 15 minutes, uninterrupted.

2. Light a blue or white candle, representing healing or peace respectively.

3. Take two or three slow, deep breaths, in through your nose, out through your mouth.

4. Say: A while back, I acted in a way that was hurtful to another. I acknowledge their pain and ask for forgiveness. I forgive myself for imperfect choices and I now release this incident from myself and let it dissolve, as it serves no purpose to remember that pain any more.

5. Allow the candle to burn until it is gone and visualize any residue of pain or regret melting away with it.

And if your grievance is against another, here is a form you can use:

I forgive _____ for their imperfect choices that caused me pain. I release them from guilt and hold the vision of their magnificent selves in my heart.

◆   ◆   ◆

Phuong* is a young professional in her late twenties who initially began working with me to sort out career choices. When she kept coming to the sessions with low energy, we began to look at what was draining her. She wasn't sleeping because she was wondering what had become of her father who had embarrassed the family by embezzling funds from his employer and later abandoned them in the middle of the night to avoid a trial. She was still hurt and angry, even though these events had taken place years before. We first looked at what the anger, the hurt and the grievance was costing her. She made a long list. Then she looked at what she was gaining from it. The major benefit wasn't much of a benefit at all: it allowed her to be the victim, which gave her an excuse to be reclusive and not develop a social life in the new city she had moved to. Over a period of weeks,

Phuong began to slowly let go of her grievance against her father. She journaled about the disappointment and anger, the fear she had felt, and the sadness the family had felt at his absence. Finally, she felt she'd said everything she wanted to say and decided to mark the occasion with a ritual of burning those pages and releasing the ashes into a river that fed into the ocean. She described feeling free of anger and sadness for the first time since her father's departure. She began to venture out to one social gathering at a time until she built a support system of loving friends and colleagues.

● ● ●

Shift the Energy with Appreciation

One way to shift the energy is to pay attention to what is working well and what you are enjoying about your life, your relationships and yourself. Remember the metaphysical law that whatever you pay attention to multiplies. If you are constantly thinking about what annoys you about someone, you may attract more of the same by giving it energy. Find something to appreciate about them instead. Everyone has qualities of merit when you look with an open mind.

> *"If you concentrate on finding whatever is good in every situation, you will discover that your life will suddenly be filled with gratitude, a feeling that nurtures the soul."*
> — **Rabbi Harold Kushner**

Of course, it is up to you to know when someone brings out the worst in you and minimize the time you spend with them. There will be people who push your buttons from your family, your friends, your coworkers and every community you are a part of. We cannot control that, but we can decide in advance to give everyone a wide margin of error, including ourselves, and let it go when it does occur.

What happens when we forgive ourselves for all past errors and abandon all grievances against anyone else is that we free up a vast amount of energy to thinking and time that can be used for more joyful pursuits.

 For Reflection

1. What are the regrets that haunt you? What does this cost you in terms of energy and happiness? How much of a relief would it be to release them?

2. What joyful pursuits will you put into the new space created?

3. Who comes to mind when you think of grievances long held?

4. What is the payoff for holding on to the hurt?

5. What will it take for you to forgive them and what would you really be giving up? What would you gain?

Look Within For Answers

The Wisdom of the Universe Resides Within You

I was at a dinner party recently where we were all talking about the books we were reading. People were animated and excited about sharing the experience of reading something particularly insightful. In the midst of this exchange, my friend and colleague got that "aha!" look and said, "I just figured out why I hang out at bookstores all the time. I'm looking for the answer!" We all laughed, and yet there was such a grain of truth to his statement that it stuck with me. We are all looking for the answers *outside ourselves*, when actually, the answer depends upon the question that only we can ask.

Obviously, I believe in the transformational power of books. After all, the one you hold in your hands was a labor of love from me to you. I don't think I would be the person I am today without the loving guidance from other authors who were willing to share their philosophy and ideas. My bias is that the best way we use information from others is to go within and ask, "Is this true for me? Does this resonate with the truth of who I am? How can this information enhance my life?" The answers that come from that kind of exploration within our own hearts and minds are our truth at that moment. It may change tomorrow or next week, but for now that is our truth as we see it.

"To know how to choose a path with heart is to learn how to follow intuitive feeling. Logic can tell you superficially where a path might lead to, but it cannot judge whether you heart will be in it."
— **Jean Shinoda Bolen**

Perhaps, then, we can begin an inquiry with a question that we are willing to sit with until answers come forth. They come in many ways. Sometimes I ask a question during my morning meditation and release it to be answered in the best way and time. Often, before the end of the day, I'll see two or three examples of the answer in different places. A simple "knowing" will pop into my mind later as I'm working on some routine task or a book will find its way to me that has a similar situation. Sometimes, it shows up in a conversation heard in a group setting that has nothing to do with me.

Your Emotional Guidance System is a Custom Design, Specific to You

If we are to discover our joy, then we must learn to navigate toward it using our feelings or emotions as tools. Often, we look around wondering how others feel about a certain event or situation and we use their emotions as our navigation, and it doesn't work, because joy is personal. What brings me delight and happiness might bore you to tears. I cannot imagine spending a beautiful Sunday afternoon in front of a television watching football or any other sport, and yet many derive great pleasure and satisfaction from that. Am I wrong? Are they? Isn't it okay that each of us decides what turns us on and what doesn't? As we begin to listen to and honor our feelings as we move through the day, adjusting here and there, we are learning to tune our dial to the channel that gives us the greatest sense of satisfaction.

"You must have a room, or a certain hour or so a day, where you don't know what was in the newspapers that morning... a place where you can simply experience and bring forth what you are and what you might be."
— **Joseph Campbell**

As I write this chapter, our nation is at war with Iraq. A lot of folks are constantly tuned in to the news channels to hear the unfolding events as they occur. To honor my own happiness, I have chosen to send peace in my daily meditations and to practice peace in my own relationships, but I do not tune in to the play-by-play description of the war. It would bring me only tension and sadness, and I do not want to lend energy to those emotions or the conflict itself. Although we might not realize it or practice it, we have a tremendous amount of choice in what we lend our energy to as we go about living our lives. Changing what doesn't work requires awareness, heartfelt desire and a willingness to experiment.

 Jack* came to see me because he had lost his spark and enthusiasm for life and wanted to find it again. He had been in the same job for over twenty years, had a good marriage of about the same length of time, a loving family, a beautiful home and was puzzled why he felt so empty. When I asked Jack about his passions, he said he didn't think he had any. Nothing really gave him a sense of excitement or anticipation. Everything looked kind of neutral to him. What we discovered over the course of our work together was that Jack was a very loving and respectful person and had allowed other people's preferences to rule his decisions for so long that he forgot what it was like to feel passion and genuine enthusiasm. I was reminded of a time when I attended a concert with a friend because her date had bailed out. The music wasn't anything that spoke to me and seemed rather bland and boring. It was the longest concert of my life and quite an enlightening experience. In Jack's case, he was so accustomed to going along with other people's choices, that he lost touch with those subtle cues that come from within that lead us down the path of delight. After doing that for so long, the fire of enthusiasm that usually burns so bright was down to a tiny, almost imperceptible flame. Jack started with small preferences to rebuild his skill at listening to those inner cues. He started with things like what movie he would like to see, what kind of restaurant he wanted to try and

what activities he wanted to include on the weekend. Gradually, that little flame got bigger and stronger and Jack began to get excited about exploring some alternative career options, and taking classes he'd always wanted to take, but no one else had shown much excitement for. Little by little, he got better at listening to and heeding his internal cues. Eventually, he drew the conclusion that he was bored doing the same thing day after day in an office and decided to reclaim his freedom. He laid out a plan for incorporating several interests into his life and creating multiple streams of income from a variety of sources so that he was experiencing more stimulation, excitement and freedom. Now, no two days are alike and he loves life more than he ever has.

●   ●   ●

The challenge many of us have in tuning in to our own inner wisdom is in slowing down and getting quiet long enough to listen. Most of us wear many hats in a day and finding twenty minutes for ourselves takes strength to say, "This time is important to me and in order to honor my highest intention, I draw a sacred circle around it." My husband and several of my clients have suggested that driving time is when they ask and listen to their inner wisdom. One friend who has a company that designs decks, told me that he used to be quite impatient on the road, since he spent so much time there. Now he looks forward to the quiet, alone time to do his best thinking. He said a side benefit was the absence of "road rage" he feels when someone cuts him off in traffic. Now, he is the observer and doesn't let that person's actions pull his attention or energy away from the creative thinking that he enjoys in this space.

> *"Just ask, 'What makes me happy, fills me with joy,*
> *or thrills me with excitement?' If you have those*
> *feelings about anything at all in your life, that is*
> *part of your guidance system telling you what to do."*
> — **Lynn A. Robinson**, in *Divine Intuition*

Learning to Ask Powerful Questions

One of the most useful tools we use in coaching is the powerful question. Clients often come to me with an issue that is causing them distress and they want immediate relief and an answer to their dilemma. But before we can arrive at that, we have to know what the scope of the challenge is. Is it one thing? Is it a combination? What is the piece that is causing the most discomfort and where is the source of that discomfort? What are the alternatives they see open to them? What other alternatives can we generate? Which one is the best fit? If I gave them a pat answer instead of helping them dig deeper and figure the answer out for themselves, it would be my answer, not theirs, and the opportunity to mine their own wisdom would be lost.

We can use powerful questions with our friends, family members, colleagues and ourselves to deepen awareness and move learning forward. The most powerful questions are open-ended and begin with What, How, or When. For example:

- What would bring me the greatest sense of delight today?

- What stops me?

- What is it that I really want to happen?

- How can I shift my perspective about this?

- How will I create a new habit that supports this shift?

- How would I like to be supported by her/him?

- When will I create these changes I have described?

- When is the best time to talk with her/him?

- When do I feel most deeply satisfied?

One of the keys to asking open-ended, powerful questions is embracing detachment. Allow your truth to be what it is without trying to manipulate the answer you'd like to hear. This requires letting go of any concern about what others might think. If you are using these kinds of questions to open a dialog with another, let go of your agenda and just hear them. That is one reason why working with a coach can net results not gained anywhere else: our only agenda is to help you get where you want to go. The other effective piece of this interaction requires listening patiently without interruption. These questions have a way of opening a door in someone's (or your own) consciousness that they didn't know was there and it is important to honor their process of discovery until they feel complete.

Questions like these are useful in gaining access to answers from within that you may not realize you have. When we get very still and quiet, there is a voice and presence within us that is wise. That voice has been with us from the beginning. Call it the voice of intuition, spirit, or deeper self. I call it the Wise Self, and have introduced many clients to listening to this voice when they think they don't know the answer. "What does your Wise Self say?" I ask them. They always pause to listen. The answer that appears comes from a deep, quiet place within. It is frequently accompanied by a long sigh or deep breath as if, finally, they can breathe easily again. Often, we are moving so fast and have so much noise and hubbub around us that we don't hear that voice. Like a feather brushing against the skin, the voice is subtle and gentle.

Cultivating a stronger relationship with this part of ourselves can give us insight into who we really are at the core. We all play a lot of roles, wear a lot of hats and we can lose touch with our own truest identity.

> *"Our lives improve only when we take chances —*
> *and the first and most difficult risk we can take is*
> *to be honest with ourselves."*
>
> — **Walter Anderson**

Exercise

Take a few unhurried moments to get in touch with your Wise Self. Finish the following statements with what feels true for you when you get quiet and look deeply at the self you are apart from all the roles you play.

- I am

- I am

- I am

- I am

- I am

- What is most important to me is

- My greatest strength is

- I want to learn more about

- I feel the greatest sense of freedom when

- I love to

♦   ♦   ♦

Looking within ourselves for answers gives us a real sense of our own power. We are the engine that powers our lives and we always know on some level what is best for us. We forget how to trust our own knowing when we listen too much to others' input or have a fear of making a mistake. Have you ever been out to dine with a friend or family member who asks everyone at the table what they are ordering, as if everyone else must have an advantage in choosing the best meal?

We are so much more than we give ourselves credit for. There lies within each of us an incredible well of wisdom to draw from. We access that wisdom by learning to get quiet and go within, where our light will astound us. Nobody "out there" knows what is better for us than our own innate intelligence. The greatest gift we give ourselves is to really experience the deeper part of who *we* are. Whatever we are looking for "out there" is already inside us or we wouldn't know to look for it.

> *"A man cannot be comfortable without his own approval."*
>
> — **Mark Twain**

In my own life, I've spent a lot of time looking for magic, music, laughter, wisdom, embracing connection, great art, great stories and God. They have all been in me the whole time. I carry them with me wherever I go and so do you. Everything you think you had to strive for was there all the time. Just like Dorothy in *The Wizard of Oz*, we dismiss the magic in our own lives, thinking we have to travel far and wide and meet a wizard to get the prize and return home. *We* are wizards and the prize is realizing our magnificence, along with everyone else's.

Our Wise Selves know what is best for us on every level: physical, emotional, spiritual. Yet, there are times when we require help accessing that part of us who knows. When we are in pain, whether emotional or physical, we may be too distracted by the pain to hear the message. Real wisdom is recognizing when to call for help, and realizing that we are constantly moving between being the giver and receiver, the healer and the healed, the teacher and the student.

When we are able to switch between giving and receiving, helping and being helped with equal grace, then we know we have grown. One of the places I've seen this manifest in my life is when I'm dining out with a friend. I grew up in a family where there was always a wrestling match over the check. "I'll get this," my Dad would say as he snatched the bill up before his friend could grab it. "No you won't! You paid last time!" his friend would counter. I replayed that scene with my own friends until I was about 35, when I really began to look at the dynamics of giving, receiving, ebb and flow. Now, when a friend wants to buy my lunch, I accept graciously, knowing the pleasure they are getting from extending their generosity and basking in the affection that prompted the offer. This feels wonderful and when I reciprocate, they accept with warmth and gratitude.

 For Reflection

1. What have you been searching for?

2. What have you tried to earn by striving?

3. What have you been seeking in other people or other places?

4. What would assist you in getting really quiet and accessing your deep wisdom?

5. What is your intention for developing the relationship with yourself?

6. What will the benefit be?

7. Which is the greater challenge for you, being the giver or receiver? How might you stretch in that area over the next month or so?

Connect to Divine Source

Allow Light and Love to Flow Freely Through You

Imagine a Divine Source that is completely loving, forgives unconditionally and sends a constant flow of energy to you and every other living being. That steady stream is filled with perfect love and light. The only things that block it are governed by us and our free will. We constrict the flow when we are angry, judgmental or unloving toward ourselves or others. Fear shuts it down to a trickle, but it is never cut off completely.

The more we consciously connect with this Divine Source the greater our access to a joy-filled life. I believe part of the longing and sadness we sometimes feel comes from the belief that we are hanging out here in life all alone, and we ache for intimacy with someone who knows us completely and loves us without condition. The desire to be known, understood and loved links us all. We all want to feel guided and supported through this adventure we're calling life. And whether we acknowledge it or not, we already have all those qualities in the relationship we have with our Source.

Some of us have almost cut ourselves off from the awareness of this loving energy because there might have been confusion and pain in our early years around the concept of a Divine Being. As adults, we get to evaluate our beliefs and decide whether they are a help or hindrance and make adjustments. Other peoples' beliefs and relationship to Divinity are not a factor unless we decide to make them a factor. We can choose to celebrate our spirituality in any way that pleases us, as no one else has power over our thoughts.

Whatever path you choose, it will be brighter, lighter and easier with your awareness of a Higher Power at your side. We are never really disconnected from our Source, yet we can be disconnected from our awareness of it. Throughout this book, many terms refer to Divinity: All-that-Is, Source, Divine Creator, the Universe, Spirit, God and many others could be used here. My belief is that we are One, born of a universal loving force. It really doesn't matter what you call that Force; they are all of the same energy—the energy of love and light. Feel free to substitute whatever name or image of God that feels most right to you, as all paths are honored and ultimately they lead each of us back to our beginning, anyway.

> *"Have hope, for My love for you will never end,*
> *nor will it ever know a limitation or a condition*
> *of any kind"*
>
> — from *Friendship With God*, by Neale Donald Walsch

There are many right ways to connect or feel the closeness of Spirit. Here are a few of the places that evoke that sense of connection:

- Watching a brilliantly colored sunset or sunrise
- Standing on a beach, feeling the power and magnitude of the ocean
- Listening to the wind blow through trees
- Holding a newborn child, as they look up at you with curiosity and trust
- Listening to music that moves you
- Enjoying a perfect rose
- Reading inspiring or uplifting prose
- Watching people embrace at the airport
- Asking a question and then getting quiet to hear the answer
- Having a stranger bestow a kindness on you

- Enjoying the beauty and power of Nature
- Acknowledging gratitude for all you have
- Seeing sweetness and generosity in someone close to you

"The same life-force that grows an oak from an acorn, a mountain from the earth's molten core, a stream from the spring thaw, a child from an egg and sperm, an idea from the mind of a human being, is present in all things, all thoughts and all experiences. There is no place where God is not."

— Joan Borysenko

We Are Never Alone

When we are paying attention, we become aware that we are really surrounded by a magnificent Force all the time. Many of us forget that part of ourselves as we get concerned about all that we are trying to be, do and have. Developing a relationship with Spirit doesn't take a lot of time or energy. In fact, it is an energy giver. There is a five-minute ritual I include in every day. Sometimes, I do it first thing in the morning before leaving the bedroom, and on days when I have early client meetings, I turn the radio off and do it on the drive to my office. The ritual is simple, yet powerful in reconnecting me to what really matters most at my core. I acknowledge the four elements and what they bring to us:

First, I acknowledge air, for bringing the breath of life, cooling breezes, the sounds of laughter, music and loved ones. Also, for inspiration and insight that comes like a breeze. I give thanks for the scattering of seeds that keep plants growing.

Then, I acknowledge the element of fire and the warmth, light, fuel, food and illumination that it brings. I think about the energy of ignition, sustaining fuel and the excitement that passion brings. I acknowledge the warmth shared between two people as we interact.

Next, I honor water in all its many forms. I am grateful for the way we are nurtured by the rain and how water refreshes us, brings adventure and fluid grace to our awareness. I think about the perfection of each snowflake and the beauty of fog. I remember how much I enjoy my morning shower, and how my dear friend, Kate, uses this as a daily metaphor: standing in the shower of abundance. I think about the example of tenacity in a stream carving out a canyon over thousands of years.

Then, my attention is turned to the element of Earth and I give thanks for her giving us all a welcome place to dwell. I give thanks for food, shelter and clothing—which all come from her generosity. I acknowledge the diversity and strength and beauty of this planet and its seasons and cycles and all they teach us.

Finally, I acknowledge the Spirit that infuses us all: every drop of dew, every bird and animal, every rock, every person. We are all connected by that Life Force. I give thanks for all the ways I'm blessed and ask for guidance for the day, and to see and feel the face of Divinity in every person I come into contact with. This only takes a few minutes, yet it helps me align with my true self. I have shifted out of some terrible moods in the space of that five-minute ritual.

Design Your Own Ritual

What kind of ritual or practice would serve you best in getting in touch with the greater awareness that is central to you? Do you enjoy rituals or reading uplifting material? Perhaps keeping a daily journal of gratitude would help you feel that connection. Allow yourself the space and acceptance to feel your spirituality in whatever way pleases you. There is no one right way. Some are going to want a formal ritual, like going to a church. That is fine for them. Others feel closer to Spirit boating on a lake. Each way is valid. Give yourself the freedom to express your Divinity in whatever brings you joy. Learn to allow others to express their Divinity in whatever way pleases them.

"Treat the other man's faith gently; it is all he has to believe with. His mind was created for his own thoughts, not yours or mine."
— Henry S. Haskins

Exercise   Sacred Space

- Look back over your life at the moments where you felt powerfully connected to your Source. Where were you? What was special about the places or times that you felt most close to Divinity?

- What was different about you?

- Where would you like to create a Sacred Space for talking to Spirit and how often would you like to connect in that way?

- What would make it easy for you to get into that mental space?

Rituals, candles, crystals, incense and music are not necessary for creating Sacred Space, but they might help you get in that mindframe, just like donning your workout gear helps get you revved up for that. What elements bring you a sense of peace and relaxation?

♦   ♦   ♦

We have access to the greatest Source of wisdom in the Universe, simply for the asking. In my coaching practice, all my clients (so far) believe in a higher power, yet many of them don't think they know how to talk with that power. They are uncertain whether the communication is two-way. Just as there are many paths that lead to Divinity, there are many right ways to communicate with your Divine Source. The key is finding or creating one that works for you. Because this is your life experience, you get to decide how, when and how frequently you want to have communication or communion with God.

"I will go before you, and make the crooked places straight."
— Isaiah 45:2

For some, meditation is the gateway. Others feel closest to their Source in nature, taking a walk in the woods or along a beach. Some like to talk as if they were talking to a close friend when driving or at other times when they have privacy and won't be interrupted. Many draw strength and peace from attending a spiritual gathering with others of like beliefs.

Why Communicate with Spirit?

The most important reason for communicating with Spirit is that we don't see the whole picture. Most of us have a limited perspective and cannot know all the circumstances or effects that a particular decision or action might have. We don't see the future or beyond our immediate past. We don't see from a "zoomed out" or objective perspective. Much of what we think is colored by our egos.

What I get from my communication with Divinity is a sense of peace. The urgency melts away as I am shown that all is well. I feel more abundant, as I am shown an unlimited supply of love and everything else required for a happy life. I feel completely loved, accepted and honored for who I am. I get a sense of playfulness and deep joy. I get healing.

Conversations with Spirit can lead to specific guidance or simply allow us to comment on something. Building any relationship takes thought and time. If you have never thought much about your relationship to God or it has been awhile since you've talked, allow it to unfold naturally and know that the interaction will be somewhat different than with others. In many conversations I've had with clients, they describe a hesitancy about starting those conversations.

One said, "It's a one-way conversation, Teri. I don't feel like I'm heard." Perhaps that's because most of us think we should get an answer in a booming voice that peals out like thunder. We do get answers, but they're usually more subtle than that. The answer may come in many forms. After getting quiet, you may hear it in your thoughts. You may pass a billboard that gives you the solution that feels right, or see it on a license plate. You may be drawn to a particular book or person later that day that provides insight you are seeking. The answer might come to you in a powerful dream or a scene in a movie. If you are willing to be open to answers coming from anyplace, the Universe can bring them much more easily and quickly. Just like anything else, at first you may feel a bit awkward talking to an unseen force. With practice, you'll develop a lasting relationship that can bring you greater clarity, peace, trust and joy than you ever imagined.

> *"Go home to your heart and you will find Me there.*
> *Unite again with your own soul, and you will unite*
> *again with Me"*
>
> — from *Friendship With God*, by Neale Donald Walsch

 Shortly after reading *Blessing: The Art and the Practice* by David Spangler, I was reminded of how much I enjoy seeing someone I don't know and sending them a blessing. I was heading home from the gym one day and stopped at a light. I looked to my left and saw a sweet-faced, young family standing at the corner, waiting for the signal to allow them to cross. The family included two young parents engaged in conversation and holding the hands of their two young children. I sent them a blessing asking that they would always have plenty of everything and be close as a family. In the moment I uttered the thought, the little girl's head snapped up and she looked right into my soul with the most dazzling smile, as if her soul heard my blessing. She shot a look of pure love and gratitude right at me. Our eyes locked for what seemed like several seconds, and that smile was huge, with one missing tooth. My eyes blurred and my heart soared, and I remembered again the power that a simple blessing can bring.

●　　　●　　　●

Be Kind to Your Body

We Are Designed to Thrive

Wholeness implies integration between emotional, physical and spiritual wellbeing. Each one is dependent upon the other for a complete sense of wellness. In order for us to fully experience our joy and follow our bliss where it leads, we must feel good in our bodies. My belief is that a healthy body begins and is sustained by a healthy mind. We are naturally whole and well until we decide, consciously or unconsciously, there is something to be gained through illness. Haven't we all had the experience of getting sick and not being able to go to some event or work that we didn't really want to do in the first place, only to have the illness magically pass after the event? So, you may be asking, if we are supposed to be perfectly healthy and thriving, why are so many of us experiencing something else?

> *"We have often heard it said that, 'We are what we eat'. But we are also what we breathe, what we think, what we say, what we see."*
>
> **— David Hoffman from *The Complete Illustrated Holistic Herbal***

What is Your Image of Self?

We begin to form an image of ourselves as soon as we arrive, based on others' response to us. We build on that with what we hear, see, experience and interpret. By the time we are entering elementary school, we have drawn some conclusions about our bodies based on what we have gathered up to then. Some of us carry those images that we created as children well into adulthood without ever challenging their validity.

If a child is told often enough that he'll catch a cold by being out in the rain and getting wet, he'll eventually believe it and make that part of his experience, until he *chooses* otherwise.

Perhaps it would be of benefit to pause and reflect on the beliefs we hold about how we get good or ill health. We are what we believe we are. If we see ourselves as energetic, we create opportunities to act that out. If we see ourselves as weak, the choices we make will be based on that assumption.

 Geoff* had experienced allergies and asthma for as long as he could remember. His family talked a lot about it, since both parents experienced similar effects. Upon beginning to explore the idea that our bodies react to our thoughts and thoughts add energy to whatever we contemplate, Geoff decided to try an experiment. He agreed to focus on all the other things that were going well—not just in his body—but in his life. He changed his habit from expecting spring allergies to expecting to feel good. He didn't talk about these conditions. He deliberately turned his thoughts to something else when his mind went there. He changed channels quickly when an allergy medication was being touted.

Eventually, Geoff's allergies and asthma disappeared. He recently said, "The ultimate test was mowing the lawn. I used to wear masks and I haven't needed them for about three years now. It's great to be able to enjoy being outside in the spring."

•　　　•　　　•

Have you ever been around someone who talked incessantly about his ills? Each time they see you, they describe yet another pain in great detail. It seems quite likely that they are attracting more pain because of their attention to it. Choose thoughts that feel good as often as you can and you lay the foundation for greater health and overall wellbeing.

A few of you may be scratching your heads right now and saying, "What's that? I can be healthier just by thinking positive thoughts?" Well, yes, you can, and not just according to me. There is a growing body of medical evidence to support these statements. Let's look at an example we can all identify with. Most everybody has heard about the placebo effect in medical experiments. This is where a number of people exhibiting the same symptom or illness is divided into groups. One group gets a new medication designed to alleviate the symptoms and the other group gets a capsule with no drug in it. Neither group knows which is which and both groups are told the drug is expected to be very successful in relieving their pain. Quite often, the group receiving the placebo experiences as much relief as the group taking the medication. Why? Because it is our *belief* that heals. Healing is in the mind. The mind is the guide and the body follows its lead.

"The natural healing force within each one of us is the greatest force of getting well."

— Hippocrates

There is great power in the belief that wellness is natural. That might be a challenge if you have been bombarded with the messages of many media ads for various medications. However, our bodies are really quite brilliant in design. Cells are constantly reinventing themselves. We slough off skin cells and reproduce new ones continually. Every few weeks, the organs we use have completely replaced themselves with brand new cells. Every part of us has been regularly upgraded since birth. Regardless of age, not one part of our bodies is very old. We are designed to thrive until the time we transition back to pure spirit. In fact, our bodies are so well designed that, with just a little kindness, they will serve us well until we are finished with them.

Exercise   Gratitude Ritual

Set aside about a half hour where you have some quiet time and will not be disturbed. This can be done on a walk, in a bath or simply sitting in a pleasant setting outdoors or inside. Take a few deep, long breaths and draw the air deep down below your belly, then blow it out, slowly through an open mouth as if you are blowing out a candle. Relax and notice how your body feels. Beginning with your feet, feel gratitude and appreciation for all the steps they have taken. You might even massage them, one at a time, as you recall a particularly demanding trek you've taken them on. Move up to your legs and knees and thank them for serving you so well. Continue in this way, remembering all the ways your body has served you and brought you pleasure. Think about all the sights, sounds, sensations and movement you have enjoyed over the years. Really appreciate, for these few moments, the gifts your body brings you. Then, ask it how you are doing at giving what it needs. Listen. You may be surprised at what you hear. Thank it for whatever it tells you and remember to honor the request, however insignificant or small it might seem. Complete this ritual as often as you like or at least twice a year, just to stay in touch with the physical part of you.

◆   ◆   ◆

Listen for What Your Body Wants

The greatest kindness you can extend to your body is to listen to its requests and honor them whenever possible. Eat when you are hungry and stop when you are satisfied. Rest when you feel like it and get some physical play when that would feel good. Our bodies send subtle cues, at first, to get our attention when we are getting out of balance. A headache might cause us to rethink those weekend plans and stay home to rest instead. If we fail to heed those subtle, quiet reminders, the volume might go up a little. How good are you at listening to and heeding your body's requests?

Sometimes I am amazed at what we expect them to endure. We wouldn't treat anyone else so shabbily. If you had a friend over and they said, "I'm thirsty, could I have a drink of water?" Would you ever think of saying, "No! You'll just want to stop and go the bathroom if I give you water now. Can't you see I'm busy?!" How often do you ignore signals to rest, to walk, to drink or eat?

 For Reflection

1. What level of health are you currently experiencing?

2. What level of health do you want?

3. Do you believe what you want is possible?

4. Are your current thought patterns more often about wellness or illness?

5. How might you shift the way you talk about your and others' health?

6. What other changes would you like to incorporate in your map for good health and a long, happy, productive life?

Our bodies are pretty good at sending accurate signals for whatever we require to feel great. The challenge is that we often override those requests. For example, how many of us only eat when we are hungry? I have learned (through *much* trial and error) to continually allow for shifts in requirements for water, food, rest and interaction according to the seasons. Here in the Pacific Northwest, our days are especially long in the spring and summer. Sometimes the sun rises around 4 a.m. and darkness doesn't fall until after 10 in the evening. During those months, our family is more active outdoors and we tend to eat more frequent, lighter meals. We especially enjoy fresh fruits and vegetables this time of year and will often have sliced cucumbers and cherry tomatoes as a mid-afternoon refreshment. The pace is faster from about April through September, then, we slow down, nap more and crave hot soups and heartier evening meals. We moved here from Texas a few years ago and adapted to this different routine fairly quickly.

Each of us is changing on an ongoing basis, and our highly sophisticated physical apparatuses are quite good at adapting. The greater challenge is accepting the attitude that change is the norm and trusting ourselves to know what we need in any given situation. This becomes easier as we learn to pause often and ask, "What do I require to feel good now?" Since each of us is a unique aspect of All-that-is, we may have different requirements and preferences about how we get movement and exercise into our routines. Wouldn't it be freeing to allow for your personal choice and never feel guilty again about abandoning the gym? There are many right ways to keep yourself active, vital and strong. Which ways appeal most to you?

 As I was enjoying a delightful massage one day, I noticed how hard my massage therapist was working. I asked, "Hillary, when you chose this career, did you know how physically demanding it would be?" She was surprised by the question, but didn't hesitate in her answer: "Yes, I did. It was a conscious choice. I wanted a profession where I would make a real difference in the quality of someone's day and I wanted to use my body in a physical way so that I don't have to use my free time working out in a gym. The bonus is that I can eat just about whatever I want whenever I want. I really like the way it worked out."

•   •   •

We require strength, vitality, stamina and energy to pursue our hearts' desires with enthusiasm. Invest a little time in lavishing affection and attention on your physical self. Experiment with movement that delights you. My husband and I love to get together with friends and dance. That doesn't feel like exercise or a chore at all. Several years ago, I discovered the pleasures of gardening and although it can be quite physically demanding, I don't notice how much energy I'm expending because it is so enjoyable to me. My husband feels the same way about golf. When we get exercise from activities we really love, it feels more like play than something we "should" do.

Be willing to try different kinds of foods and design a routine around your unique timing. I used to enjoy eating popcorn when we rented a movie. Then, I began to awaken in the night with a dry mouth and swollen fingers after eating popcorn. The salt wasn't agreeing with me. An interesting substitution that I now really enjoy is dry flax cereal. It has a nutty taste and satisfying crunchy texture. My body seems quite pleased with this change. Sometimes, it seems we eat more for entertainment than nourishment. Try choosing foods based on how energetic or good they let you feel.

If you have experienced challenges with good health, be patient with yourself. We are often not taught about the effects our thoughts have on our health. Our American culture is filled with messages that teach us to expect a decline in good health as we age. Deepak Chopra says that we are "under the hypnosis of social conditioning." In his work, *Magical Mind: Magical Body*, Chopra talks about several studies on aging conducted by Harvard scholars and researchers. In countries where age is venerated rather than dreaded, people have quite a different experience. For example, in some African cultures, growing older is believed to be equivalent to growing better. Older people are seen as wiser, more capable and given greater responsibility. They hold the most important positions in business and community, and are respected for their greater length of experience. Runners in their sixties perform better than their young counterparts. These studies concluded that the societal expectation of aging plays a major role in determining what people experience.

Let us use this evidence to collectively change our expectations about health and aging. If we genuinely anticipate life getting better and better as we go along, it must. Breaking old habits is not easy. We give ourselves permission to begin again every day. Gradually, we learn new ways to support our wellness and growth. When we treat ourselves with kindness and lovingly tend our needs, we make a powerful shift in the way we experience life.

Honor Your Values

What's Important to You?

I had a conversation with a friend recently who had decided definitely not to have children. She was apologetic in her description, and she wrapped it up something like this: "I just finally decided that I love my work, I like my life just the way it is and I'm not really willing to give up anything to have children. Do you think I'm incredibly selfish?"

"Yes," I answered. "And rightly so. Who better to decide what is best for you than you?" So often we muddle the decisions we make about our own lives by trying to please the world. It can't be done. The best any of us can do is live our lives fully and joyfully and to do that, we must know what is important to us—no matter how it might look to anybody else. My friend had some values at play that she decided were important to honor. She enjoys her career and gets satisfaction from that. She and her husband like being able to travel on short notice. They enjoy eating out and aren't particularly interested in cooking. In her free time at home, she loves making her home sparkle and likes it to stay that way. She enjoys being an aunt and playing with nieces and nephews and that satisfies her desire to be with children. The only discomfort she was feeling about the decision she made was the disappointment she anticipated from parents and other family members. They chose to have children; she didn't. It is as simple as that.

Each of us has the right and the *responsibility* to choose what makes us happy.

> *"Again and again we have seen clients make decisions based on their bank balance, or their fear of creating discomfort or their worry about others' displeasure. They make decisions based on what is easiest at the moment or decisions that minimize the size of the waves. Such decisions never work out for their fulfillment because they have sold out on themselves and their values."*
>
> — from ***Co-Active Coaching***

What are the things that are most important to you, in terms of being, doing and having? What are the values that guide your life— not what you think *should* be important, simply those that *are* important? If you haven't gotten clear enough to write them down, you might find some surprises when you do. Our deeply held values are the things that drive us, consciously or unconsciously. If we know what they are, we can make decisions that are in harmony with what we hold dear. For example, I know that freedom is a top value for me, so any decision I make is considered from that point of view. I have almost always chosen work that allowed me to set my priorities, choose projects, design schedules and decide parameters. I like having the freedom to decide in the moment what to do. My number one value is wellbeing on a physical, spiritual and emotional level. If there needs to be any adjustment to maintain that, it takes precedence. When an invitation comes along, I look to see how it fits in with what's most important to me before responding. Nurturing relationships is pretty high up for me, so if I can accept the invitation without violating my wellness, I'll usually say yes. If I'm already heavily scheduled and accepting the invite would be taxing, I'll say no and do not feel a smidgeon of guilt.

"Our values serve as a compass pointing out what it means to be true to oneself. When we honor our values on a regular and consistent basis, life is good, life is fulfilling."

— from **Co-Active Coaching**

Sometimes, there is a shift in what is most important to us on any given day. If we're feeling burned out, we might be ready for some rest and relaxation. Sitting by the pool and reading might sound delightful. Once we're rested, that might not be enough stimulation. Just like there is an ebb and flow to the tides, we are constantly shifting and changing and making adjustments to what we want in the current moment. That desire is what summons Life Force to move through us, and we will always have a new desire.

Exercise   Value Assessment

To get an idea of what your top priorities are, take a look at the following list and mark those that you feel are important. Then, return to the list and choose your personal top ten. Rank them in importance to you, one being the most important. These are your core values, and they have likely been with you for life. Knowing them will assist you in making choices that honor your deepest self.

If you have a life partner, you might want to copy this exercise for them and compare. Knowing what is most important to your partner will allow you to honor them in a very supportive and loving way.

What's Important to You?

Accomplishments	Excitement	Pleasure
Accountable	Expertise	Potential
Achievement	Faith	Power
Accuracy	Fame	Privacy
Acknowledgment	Family	Public Service
Admiration	Fast Living	Purity

Advancement	Fast-pace work	Recognition
Adventure	Financial gain	Renewal
Aesthetics	Freedom	Results
Altruism	Friendship	Risk taking
Arts	Fun	Romance
Autonomy	Generosity	Resonance
Balance	Gratitude	Responsible
Beauty	Honesty	Right livelihood
Bliss	Humor	Security
Bonding	Independence	Self-expression
Calm	Influence	Self-respect
Challenges	Inner harmony	Sensuality
Change	Integrity	Serenity
Clarity	Intellectual challenge	Service
Collaboration	Intimacy	Sharing
Commitment	Involvement	Simplicity
Communication	Job tranquility	Solitude
Community	Joy	Spirituality
Compassion	Knowledge	Stability
Competence	Leadership	Status
Competition	Learning	Time
Completion	Love	Trust
Connecting	Loyalty	Truth
Contribution	Magic	Understanding
Creativity	Mastery	Vitality
Decisiveness	Merit	Wealth
Detachment	Mindfulness	Wholeness
Economic security	Money	Will
Efficiency	Nature	Wisdom
Emotional health	Openness	Wonder
Energy	Order	Working alone
Entrepreneurial	Partnership	Working w/others
Environment	Patience	_____
Ethical practice	Personal growth	_____
Excellence	Physical challenge	_____

◆   ◆   ◆

You have a very sophisticated guidance system in your emotions. When you are honoring your values, you feel great. Happiness and wellbeing flow freely. When you are not acting or thinking in harmony with your greater self, your guidance system offers negative emotion to get your attention so that you may stop and realign. Sometimes we just keep choosing the same things and feeling the negative emotion because it has become a habit and we have not been taught that those emotions are an indicator to look for misalignment.

For instance, if you have a high value for orderliness and yet your surroundings continue to be disorderly, you might feel yourself getting cranky or distracted. If solitude is important for your wellbeing and you are constantly with people, you may feel hostile toward them until you get away and fill that requirement for solitude for awhile. When you feel yourself getting out of sorts, stop and ask, "What need do I have that is not being met. What do I want?"

"The heart has its reasons which reason knows not of."
— Pascal

Many of my clients have expressed that they love being outdoors, yet they work in jobs where they are behind a desk, drive to and from work in a car, go home and cook, cleanup, fall into bed and do it all again the next day. If you love being outdoors, honor that in yourself by creating opportunities to be outdoors. You have come here to this life to have the best possible experience you can create, and you really are a powerful creator, made in the likeness of the Divine Creator. Allow yourself to design what pleases you. You do not have to "settle for" anything. That is scarcity-based thinking, and if you are on a path to joy, you will want to release all limits. Begin today to notice what is important to you and honor that in every way you can.

 Kaitlin* was a regional sales director for a high tech firm and spent much of her week on flights to cities where she hopped from meeting to meeting and back again. Reports and then

more meetings followed to the tune of about 70 hours a week. One result was that her health had begun to decline. Her blood pressure was far above normal.

Before we began our work together, Kaitlin had been acting as if her number one value was financial and job security. When she identified her top ten values, it turned out that emotional wellbeing was number one. This allowed her to see where not honoring her true priorities had pulled her off balance and she was then able to begin restructuring her work and life in a way that allowed her to take care of her needs and wants without sacrificing what was most important. The interesting thing was, once she made that commitment to herself, things began shifting in her organization and lined up in a way that supported the changes she wanted to make. Many of those shifts occurred without her having to *do* anything. Amazing things happen when we get clear about our intentions.

• • •

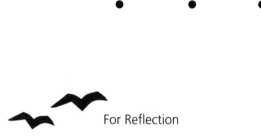 For Reflection

1. How would your activities change if you made decisions based on your core values?

2. What relationships, events, obligations or objects would you like to let go of?

3. What would you want to move into that vacated space, if anything?

Sometimes, we allow ourselves to be pressured into doing things that we'd really prefer not to do. This is especially true around the winter holidays. Many people buy gifts even though they don't really want to. Some make long pilgrimages to participate in gatherings they find no pleasure in. It takes courage to say, "We've decided to start our own traditions in our home this year," knowing that you might get a cold shoulder from someone you love. Family and friends may be shocked to learn that you'd really rather travel to an exotic location for exploration than do another gift exchange by the tree. They *will* get over it.

Give from a Genuine, Heartfelt Desire

When we let other peoples' preferences become more important than our own, we run the risk of not knowing the joy of our own freedom. I am not suggesting that we never do something for the sake of giving pleasure to someone else—I am stating that we would serve them and us better if the gesture comes from a true desire to give and not feeling that we "should." When we feel like we are sacrificing what we really want in order to give to someone else, they feel it, too. Stop and ask yourself, "Am I doing this from the heart, because I want to?" If the answer is yes, then you and the receiver will be blessed by the gesture. If the answer is no, you may feel resentment that you had to give something up for them, and they are likely to detect your resentment and return it to you.

> *"Does this path have a heart? If it does, the path is good; if it doesn't, it's of no use."*
> — Carlos Castaneda

Often, married couples or others in long-term relationships begin to feel resentment after a few years because they each have compromised more than they really wanted to. My husband and I each grew up in families that honored the tradition of eating together. Early in our marriage, this created a bit of a struggle. While we both enjoy sitting down to share a meal, it simply doesn't work for us during the week. He is up and out the door to a more traditional job at an early hour. In the mornings, I simply have no appetite until at least 8:30. We jointly decided that we would honor our own timing in this and other areas. I like to work out at different times of day, but by evening, my energy level and interests have shifted and I have no interest in going to the gym. He enjoys going for a workout at around 7 p.m. In every relationship, there are preferences and natural tendencies on each side. There are individual values to be honored. Allow yourselves the freedom to live according to what is important to you. Besides, if we do everything else together, what on earth will we talk about when we finally do sit down to dinner with each other? When two people each live vibrant, fulfilling lives according to their own desires, their coming together is more of a celebration; each of them is full of life and eager to share their experiences with the other. Each one is enriched by the variety and different points of view.

When you first begin to incorporate some of these changes, friends and family members may balk and even pout with you. Let them know in a gentle and loving way that you are learning to honor your own personal needs and give them permission to do the same. It seems ridiculous to expect that, just because we love someone and choose them for a life partner we would want to do everything together, yet our culture sometimes portrays this as the norm for people in love.

Become an Allower

Live and Let Live

What is an allower? An allower is one who accepts and even embraces her whole self and others just as they are. He realizes that only his own reaction is under his control and doesn't waste energy trying to control other people or situations. She makes the best of any situation, looks for the positive aspects of that situation and focuses on what she wants, not from a viewpoint of lack, but from a place of appreciation.

Giving ourselves permission to be who we naturally are takes away resistance and life becomes more fluid. Abundance, prosperity, things and situations can all flow to us more easily. By the same token, when we give ourselves the room to be who we really are, we invite others to do the same. In addition we let Spirit and situations be what they are. This is truly a great gift. You may have noticed that those who make it a practice in their lives are extremely attractive to all they desire. We all appreciate the breathing room to relax and be ourselves. Being with someone who accepts us wholly is like putting on a comfortable bathrobe and breathing a sigh of relief. The tension simply melts away and pretty soon we feel the warmth and companionship that let's us laugh together.

When we meet people who embrace this philosophy, we remember them for the way they make us feel: free. They will say things like, "Let me know when you're ready to try that restaurant and we'll go together." No pressure, no worries. They give themselves and us ample space to move about.

There's a very subtle but important difference between being an allower and being a tolerator. When we give ourselves freedom to think, behave and express at an authentic level, we naturally follow our own happiness wherever it takes us. We aren't tolerating something we find less than appealing, but are actually embracing and trusting ourselves at a deeper level. When we genuinely grant this same freedom to others we are embracing and trusting them. Tolerating, on the other hand, is when we see things we don't like and are annoyed by them, but we keep silent about it.

> *"A loving person lives in a loving world. A hostile person lives in a hostile world. Everyone you meet is your mirror."*
>
> — **Ken Keyes, Jr.,** ***Handbook of Higher Consciousness***

Offer Suggestions Only When Asked

Most of us have been around well-intentioned friends and family who offer advice and suggestions on how we might change. Even though the underlying basis might be one of love and concern, this kind of offering usually comes across as criticism and isn't generally well received. When we become allowers, we don't necessarily offer up suggestions for changing or critiquing someone else's behavior unless they ask for that.

 Doug* and Suzanne* had been in many rounds of conflict with their twenty-something daughter, Amy. Every time she came home from college, the battle of wills began. Suzanne could feel the tension gathering in her shoulders when Amy left clutter in every room and she saw her husband's jaw clench. In coaching, they agreed to try an experiment. They would anticipate rather than dread Amy's next visit. When they thought of her being home, they would focus on the part of her visit they really enjoyed: cooking together, the vivid and colorful stories she tells about her college

friends and characters, different outings they would go on. When Amy arrived, Doug and Suzanne were thrilled to see her and she responded with genuine enthusiasm. As she dropped backpacks and bags in the hall, her Dad put his arm around her shoulder and said, "I'll help you carry that stuff upstairs later, but right now we want to hear all about what's been going on with you...we can't wait to hear your stories about the characters you hang out with." Amy's eyes shone, and she said, "Really? Well, have I got a good one for you...." They had a wonderful visit. Doug and Suzanne kept flowing love and appreciation to their daughter and Amy sensed the appreciation her parents were feeling toward her. As a result, she was more meticulous about keeping things tidy than she had ever been. Their time together as a family was joyful and stress free.

•   •   •

What does it look like when a person is an allower? Well, in the relationship with themselves, they don't make apologies for their preferences or their choices. They honor those choices and embrace the whole of who they are. They enjoy – even milk— every situation for all the pleasure, joy and contentment they can get from it. As an allower of others, they can be with those they don't necessarily agree with, yet appreciate the difference in perspective. They give that person the freedom to be their whole selves without the need to justify their choices or pretend to be something else. The acceptance they offer for themselves and others creates the safety to show up authentically. That gives the relationship space to grow, because the other person feels like they are unconditionally accepted. When others know they won't be judged, criticized or belittled for their choices, an attitude of mutual respect and gratitude is created and becomes a solid foundation for the relationship to blossom at a higher level. It gives all parties the space to experiment and say, "Let me try this out with you." This can be in the form of conversation, wardrobe, roles or freethinking ideas. That safe space allows for creative playfulness and experimentation without fear of reprisal.

This open mindset also gives permission for Spirit to speak and communicate with us more freely than before. We make room for possibilities that we can't see. It's almost like there's a window we're looking through— a window to our lives—and we can see straight ahead and to this side and that side, but we can't see the whole picture. There is a broader, unlimited perspective in the spiritual realm and when we trust and allow that intelligence to communicate with us, we're giving ourselves and Spirit the freedom to have a broader view and allow for possibilities that we might not think of on our own. We make room for something wonderful to come into our lives that we might love but never thought to ask for.

As I write this chapter, it's mid-summer in the year 2003. We find ourselves in a world that is very different than what it was a few years ago. These are interesting and challenging times because the economy here in the United States seems to be a little shaky; we are at war and our relationship with other countries has been compromised in some ways. Everybody has an idea of what they think should be happening. Sometimes what's really happening and what we want to happen are quite different.

When we embrace the allowing mindset even in situations this extreme, where world events are affecting each of us on some level, we can come to a place where we let the world be what it is. We make room for the intelligence of the universe. What does that mean? It means holding a sense of trust that things will right themselves if given a chance and embracing peace in our hearts. Let's take a look at how this might show up in a person's daily life.

Where Will You Focus Your Energy?

One thing to consider is not overdosing on bad news. Be a little more selective about what is allowed into your experience as far as radio, television and news. Decide consciously what thoughts you are willing to entertain. Would you knowingly choose thoughts of war, a bad economy or gloom and doom? These have been aspects of every generation, and each person makes a decision about how much of their personal thought and energy they are willing to give to these stories. Would you like to turn your attention away from those and put your energy toward more uplifting aspects? Those are out there too, and we can focus on whichever thoughts we choose to. By embracing the more positive aspects and getting in harmony with those, we're more likely to be in tune with our higher selves.

Allow Your Desires to Come

This is the recipe for bringing whatever you're trying to manifest into your life, whether it is the quality of peace, harmony, joy or something more tangible, like a new home. It's the step that I think most of us get a little hung up on because it's so simple and we have ingrained habits of thinking patterns. Here's an example: you want a new car and you're pretty sure that you'd like for it to be a convertible coupe in a bright color. You see yourself driving in the summer with the breeze in your hair and how much you're going to enjoy this car on the road. You can feel the pleasure it's going to bring you and the appreciation for how much more reliable it will be than the old rattletrap that you might be driving now. You get very clear and specific, ask for it and get excited about having it. At this point you are attracting that new car, because you are vibrating the joy of having it. But then a couple of weeks down the road you start thinking, "Well where is it? It hasn't shown up yet." Part of the allowing process is to know when to let go of the outcome. You have gotten clear about what you want and you've asked for it; now trust it's coming and don't let doubt creep in. When you doubt, you're resisting, not allowing. Allowing is really a sense of trust that things are going to come in their perfect time.

Allowing is also trusting that others are creating exactly what they want to create. They have the right to make the choices they're making and live the life they're living. They know what they want better than anyone else could.

Trust Your Loved Ones to Make Choices that Serve Them

One place where we have a great challenge in the allowing of others is in our immediate circle of friends and family. This likely comes from a sense of love and wanting to help and yet our interference may be misguided. We look at someone in our life and see the choices they're making and the results they're getting and that they don't seem very happy. We think if we step in and tell them what we're seeing and give them some ideas and our point of view, they might want to do it differently. The truth is, we're all very wise and connected with our spiritual sides and each of us has a very knowing inner self that we can draw wisdom and discernment from. If that person is making a choice that's not bringing them the results they want, there may be something they're choosing not to look at; or they may be doing it that way for a very specific reason that we know nothing about.

It can be a challenge to look at someone else's life and allow them to have their pain, their dysfunctional romantic relationships, their illnesses or their emotional upheavals. Especially with our children, it is difficult to let them to have their financial woes, and trust them that sooner or later they'll either figure it out or do something different.

> *"If you want to be free, there is but one way; it is to guarantee an equally full measure of liberty to all your neighbors. There is no other."*
>
> — Carl Schurz

Being an allower is having a sense of trust about ourselves. We can say, "I know what I'm doing. I know what I want and it might be different tomorrow, but today I know this is what I want and these are the steps I'm choosing to give attention to and these are thoughts I have about it and this is how I'm feeling about it emotionally. I'm excited and eagerly anticipating." When we embrace this for ourselves, we naturally want to give everyone else that same freedom.

Be Open to Receive Wisdom from Unexpected Places

One of the places that I draw inspiration from is a non-physical group of teachers called Abraham, channeled through Esther Hicks. They offer a beautiful analogy about life: the world is like a lovely kitchen that is equipped with every ingredient you can imagine. Each of us is making a pie that represents our life — we're working on perfecting the recipe for our pie. We're tasting and testing and baking and tasting and testing and baking and we add a little bit of this and a little bit of that, then someone comes along and says, "Oh, no! No! You're doing it all wrong! You don't want to put that in your pie – that'll ruin your pie. You ought to do it this way." We stand back, look at them and think, "You know, I really had a pretty good pie before you ever came along. I was just adding a little and testing a little and perfecting it. I really didn't want somebody to come up and tell me to start all over with my recipe."

Making assumptions about how people are experiencing their lives is presumptuous, because the way we perceive them and the way they really experience it may be completely different. Allow yourself and everyone else to have whatever experiences each of you wants and trust that you *can't* get it wrong.

Exercise

Think about someone in your life who has a challenging situation they've been grappling with, where you've been itching to give advice and would like to see them use your ideas for solving this challenge they're facing.

- What are the aspects of their situation that you might not know about? What are the possibilities they might be grappling with that are not visible to you?

- What would be the value of them resolving this issue on their own – with their own resources, their own mind, their own ideas?

- What would you be taking away from them by swooping in like Superman and trying to change it for them?

- What would the non-verbal message be that you'd be sending if you tried to do that?

Is that the kind of person you want to be? Is that the kind of contribution you want to make to them?

♦   ♦   ♦

 When I was training for my certification in coaching several years ago, I remember being frustrated in one of our exercises. We were paired with another student and one of us played coach, one played client. The client was asked to describe a challenge they were currently grappling with. The coach was to ask powerful questions and allow the client to come up with their own solutions. Sometimes this meant a few moments of silence while the client was processing their thoughts. It took all of my self-control to keep from entering that space of silence with my bright ideas. I learned a powerful lesson that week: when clients arrive at their own solutions, they have come from a place deep inside them and the process itself is immensely valuable. Additionally, when they own the solution, they're much more committed to seeing it through. We all love to see our ideas in action. The exercises we had in training that week mirror the kinds of conversations we have every day with people we care about.

●　　　　●　　　　●

 For Reflection

1. How much room do you give yourself to pursue whatever calls you without worrying how it might appear to others?

2. Who are the people in your life that challenge you most and how could you allow them to be who they are and still honor who you are?

3. Where would you like to stretch, relative to becoming more of an allower?

Release Fear and Embrace Trust

As observers of nature, we see the role of fear in a different light than when looking at ourselves or each other. Animals only seem to experience fear when there is a known threat—as a predator approaches, for example. They appear to go into a sharper alertness, becoming keenly aware of all movement and sound around them. They size up the situation and take action to avoid harm by fleeing, hiding or fighting. When it's over, they go back to enjoying life the way they did before the interruption. They embrace trust and go about their business. You won't see an animal take to strong drink or join a support group over something that frightened them momentarily. They live in the moment.

> *"You have powers you never dreamed of. You can do things you never thought you could do. There are no limitations in what you can do except the limitations of your own mind."*
> — **Darwin P. Kingsley**

Fear Can Be a Useful Tool

How different our experience of life would be if we only felt fear in times of imminent danger. In looking back over my life, there have only been a few times there was any real threat to me, but many times I allowed fear to run free with my thoughts. Suppose for a moment that fear is really a message from our intuition alerting us to be more aware so that we can avoid harm. That's a useful device. It worked for me one afternoon as I returned home from college classes and entered the garage. Before I ever got out of the car, the hair on the back of my neck was standing and I felt quite strongly that something was amiss. I approached the back door slowly, entering the kitchen with a sense of wariness. Upon turning my head as I took one step in, I saw the shattered glass of our patio door and the firewood someone had used to break it. Immediately, I returned to the car, and went to alert the police station. Before I was a block away from the house, a police car appeared and I waved him over. Upon returning to the house, we discovered that the burglars had likely left out of the front door as they heard the garage door open in the back. They had emptied half of my jewelry case and fled. That day, my intuition alerted me to be aware. I believe that is the true purpose of fear.

> *"We cannot escape fear. We can only transform it into a companion that accompanies us on all our exciting adventures. Take a risk a day — one small or bold stroke that will make you feel great once you have done it."*
>
> **— Susan Jeffers**

Choose Thoughts that Feel Good

The other times we feel fear is when we *imagine* all sorts of possible future catastrophies. That is not very helpful, yet it's a place where many of us live. There are people who allow their thoughts to turn to all kinds of possible disasters and play them out mentally, scene by scene. This has an extremely negative affect on their outlook, attitude and health. Constant worry causes stress to the body, mind and spirit. As far as I can tell, it does nothing positive for us at all.

We can learn new patterns of thought and behavior that allow us to move through our lives with greater health, satisfaction and joy. That is the purpose of this book: to assist you in shifting up to a fuller, more joyful experience. One way to do that is to embrace trust by noticing all the good in your life.

Often, people take for granted all the many ways their life is working well and fixate on the one area that doesn't measure up to their expectations. They hold a magnifying glass to that one spot and things begin to heat up. Remember that we are constantly attracting according to our thoughts. When we look at some flaw, pretty soon we attract a lot of other very similar thoughts. We attract other people who are thinking or experiencing along those lines. We attract more of whatever it is we find so distasteful, simply because we are lending it our very powerful focused energy and attention.

Look For Positive Aspects of Each Situation

One way to diffuse fear and anxiety is to keep things in perspective and put down the magnifying lens. In other words, pay attention to all the areas of your life, not just the one that feels out of whack. For instance, many of my clients over the last couple of years were affected by layoffs and very fearful about having enough money and finding their next job opportunity. When we worked together to create a healthy plan for moving forward, they took a more balanced view of their lives and began to look at other aspects they could give positive attention to. They agreed to take excellent care of their bodies, acknowledging that good self-care was an investment in wellbeing that would pay off in terms of greater energy, reduced anxiety and a more positive outlook.

 Ben* was a stressed-out technical illustrator who had been spending every waking moment looking for work. By the time he met with me, was discouraged and fighting low energy and depression. He was extremely fearful about many aspects of his future, particularly replacing his job and repairing his marriage. Although he questioned the merit of spending less time on the job search (he actually thought he should be spending *more* than 40 hours a week on it), he agreed to try a few ideas and see how they worked. He began taking daily walks with his wife. He finally had time to clean out the garage and organize his tools and art supplies they way he'd wanted to for years. Then, he tackled

the back yard, which had become overgrown and weedy. He spent part of each day taking steps to find the right career opportunity and maintain balance and progress in all other areas. After a few weeks, his whole attitude changed. He reported having greater clarity about what was really important to him. His relationship with his wife was dramatically improved as they were communicating on their daily walks in a way they had not for many years. This led to healing a painful break in trust that had haunted their relationship for some time. He felt a sense of pride and accomplishment at all the home projects he was completing and his energy and enthusiasm were returning. He was getting re-acquainted with his teenaged son after many years of seventy-hour workweeks, where he saw very little of him or anyone else at home. In short, Ben turned his thoughts and attention to other positive aspects of his life while continuing with a comfortably paced job search. By fully taking advantage of this time and keeping a balanced approach to all areas of his life, not only did Ben greatly reduce his fear, he gained much greater clarity about the parameters he wanted to honor. Not long after, he attracted a new position that allowed him the work-life balance and satisfaction he had always wanted.

•   •   •

Each of us is multidimensional, yet we tend to forget that when we allow fear or concern for one area to overshadow everything else.

 For Reflection

We are so much more alike and connected than we realize. Take a look at these common areas where fear resides for many of us:

1. Health (physical, mental, spiritual, for ourselves and others)

2. Relationships (to self, to God, to others and how they see us)

3. Money and Career (making the "right" choices, being enough, having enough)

4. World Conditions (extreme weather, earthquakes, wars, economic concerns)

Begin to look for areas that are working in each of these categories. Ask:

1. What parts of your physical body are working well?

2. What mental abilities are serving you just fine?

3. How many of your friends, loved ones and colleagues are well?

4. What are the relationships that are working well in your life?

5. Where is there abundance in your life?

6. What aspects of your work are pleasing to you?

7. What is working well in your community? Your state? Your country? Your planet? Your solar system? Your universe?

Look for What Pleases You

We are so accustomed to looking for what is *not* working, we often forget the magnitude of what is going very well for all of us. Begin now to embrace trust. Foster a greater sense of trust in your own potential and abilities. Be more trusting of others. We often sense whether or not those in our lives believe in us, and that gives us the momentum we need to keep going. Believe in the basic goodness of yourself and everyone else. Trust your intuition to guide you and trust your Divine Creator to support you. Let "All is well" become your daily mantra.

"Set your intention, and trust the universe to take care of the details."

— **Mike Fotheringham**

Exercise

Each of us has an internal picture about the way things are that governs our behavior. Begin to notice whether your internal picture points to the odds being stacked in your favor or against you. Over the next week, choose one or two of the following questions to ponder over a day's activity, and write your observations in your journal.

- In general, do I feel like life is going to get better as I go along or that I have to hold on very hard to keep from losing what I have?

- As I start out on an errand, do I have a mental picture of things going smoothly?

- What am I expecting as I make my way to work in the morning? Do I see the day unfolding the way I'd like it to or am I fixating on a problem or person that is perplexing?

- Do I generally expect people to like and appreciate me? Or do I anticipate conflict?

- What is my view about money and having enough? Do I enjoy exchanging my money for things that please me or do I resent having to let go of my hard-earned cash?

After a week or so of just noticing your thoughts about these questions, you will begin to see a pattern emerge. There will likely be things you are quite trusting about and other things you are more fearful about. Allow yourself to take small steps toward a more trusting and optimistic view. Ask what view would serve you best. You have amazing power in your thoughts and the free will to choose anything you desire. Choose thoughts that support the kind of life you want to live, and release those that do not assist you.

♦   ♦   ♦

"You may have a fresh start any moment you choose, for this thing we call failure is not the falling down, but the staying down."

— **Mary Pickford**

Acknowledge and Express Gratitude

Gratitude Opens Many Doors

There may be no faster route from discouragement to joy than through gratitude. When we express heartfelt appreciation for anything, we experience an upward shift in our energy. Sometimes I grumble about getting up and going for a walk on days when it seems so tempting to stay in that warm, cozy bed. However sluggish I might be at the start, I have discovered that when I walk with a sense of discovering something to appreciate, I see magic along the way. Maybe it's the fog that makes everything look soft and dreamy. In the summer, it is fascinating to see the sun burning off the fog. It evaporates right before my eyes. Once, I discovered a perfectly designed, dew-covered spider web glowing like a crystal in the sunlight. Occasionally, I've heard the sound of bull frogs on the pond. I always return from those walks feeling energized and refreshed by the air, the myriad sights and sounds of nature and the feeling of wonder I get when alone on a walk.

Once we discover the power that comes from acknowledging what we are truly grateful for, it becomes more a way of living than anything else. Often in our society, we learn to be objective: to weigh the pros and cons of every situation or decision. While often useful, this teaches us to look for the downside or the flaws in everything. Although there may be merit in using this kind of thinking for things like quality control, or choosing the best car for your needs, the behavior easily becomes a habit—a sort of lens we look through that crosses over into our relationships and every other facet of life. Eventually, we become conditioned to look for what is wrong with every person, object or event we are exposed to. If that goes unchecked, it isn't long before the first and only thing we see about anything is what is wrong with it.

"If the only prayer you say in your life is "thank you," that would suffice."
— Meister Eckhart

Remember the first time you fell in love, and how wonderful that person appeared to you in the early stages of your relationship. After a while, we aren't as willing to overlook little annoyances and if we allow it, we can focus on those to the degree that they are all we notice. Where once our faces lit up upon seeing this one, we now say, "Oh, it's you," when they enter a room. Now we forget the warmth in their eyes and how much we like to laugh together because we're focused on whether or not they are going to do that thing again that drives us crazy.

Or, we arrive at a lovely hotel on a trip where everything is top notch. The staff is friendly, the food is delicious, the beds are comfortable. Oh, but that shower makes an awful whining noise, so we focus on that and complain about it and then we begin looking for other things like that, until pretty soon we have made a convincing argument that this is a sub-par hotel and we'll never stay here again. If these scenes sound familiar, it is because most of us experience similar ones many times each day.

Look For Things to Appreciate

Begin to develop the habit of looking for the positive aspects in every person and every situation and you will notice a major shift occurring in your life. Your energetic vibration literally changes as you turn your thoughts to what you appreciate.

Start with yourself. What do you most appreciate about you? Maybe you like your quirky sense of humor or the way you are able to put people at ease.

*"Appreciation is a wonderful thing: It makes what
is excellent in others belong to us as well."*
— Voltaire

As soon as you hear a self-criticism in your mind, steer your thoughts in another direction by saying, "OK, that is something I would do differently next time, but what do I appreciate about the way I handled the rest of that situation?" Use this same pivoting technique the next time you find yourself mentally bashing someone else. Granted, they may have some annoying qualities...we all do. It's easy to spot those. If you look a little deeper, what are the aspects of that person you genuinely appreciate? Wouldn't you want others to consider the whole package and not just measure you by your objectionable behavior?

Here is an example: my husband is a real treasure in many ways...being a snappy dresser isn't one of them. He cleans up good, and looks very presentable when we go out or when he is at a business meeting. When we are just lounging at home, though, he is quite happy to wear flannel pants and a well-worn tee shirt. This used to bother me, until I thought about the positive aspects of it: no matter what I'm wearing, he tells me I'm beautiful and makes me feel completely loved and accepted. He is just as drawn to me in sweats as he is when I wear a sexy dress. Part of his charm is that he sees past the clothing to the person inside, and it's one of the things I love most about him. So, I decided the positive aspects far outweighed my preference for a sharper image and decided to focus on what I appreciate. The more I do this with people and situations, the more pleasurable life becomes. If we need anyone to change so that we can be happy, then our happiness will always be dependent upon the decisions of others.

*"Gratitude is our most direct line to God and the
angels. The more we seek gratitude, the more reason
the angels will give us for gratitude and joy to exist
in our lives."*
— Terry Lynn Taylor

One way to begin making this shift into noticing the things that we feel thankful for is to start a gratitude journal. I use a small spiral notebook that sits on top of my desk. At the end of my workday, I jot down the people I was with and what I appreciated about them. There are usually other aspects that come to mind as I mentally replay the highlights. Only positive aspects go in this journal and entries might look like this:

- I enjoyed my voice lesson with Celeste; she really got into the Louis Armstrong song with me and we laughed 'til our faces hurt.

- All the lights were green on my way to the office. That was cool!

- It was fun shopping with Annie. Her wacky sense of humor always cracks me up and I appreciate her sense of style.

- I love working with my new client! Never met anyone like him before. What an interesting life.

- Got an unexpected refund from a credit card company. Yeah!! Time to shop again.

We can literally feel our mood, emotions and vibrations lift as we focus on the things that bring us pleasure. When we find reasons to celebrate often, life gets better and better. This morning, a client brought me a gift from Japan. She knows I love cats and it is a solar-powered kitty that waves. She told me it represents success in business and many Japanese businesses have a cat in that posture in their offices to bring prosperity. I was delighted to receive the gift and will feel appreciation for this client each time I see it. Little things add immeasurably to our experience every day.

Every once in a while, as I look back over my entries, I feel so fortunate and blessed to have so many positive, uplifting moments in my life. I am not unique or special. All of us have them. Some of us have simply formed a habit of tuning in to the less positive aspects. The good news is that no one else chooses your thoughts and you can change your tuner any time you decide to. Imagine there are two stations broadcasting. One feels good and one feels bad. You are responsible for setting your dial to receive the station you want to hear, just as you are responsible for transmitting thoughts that feel good when you think them.

> *"Happiness cannot be traveled to, owned, earned, worn or consumed. Happiness is the spiritual experience of living every minute with love, grace and gratitude."*
> **— Denis Waitley**

 For Reflection

1. What are the physical attributes you appreciate about yourself? Emotional attributes? Mental abilities? Characteristics and skills?

2. Who are the people that most add pleasure to your life experience and what do you love about them?

3. If you have animal companions, what do you most love about them?

4. What points of nature do you find to be most beautiful and inspiring?

5. What opportunities have come your way in life that you feel gratitude for?

6. What else are you thankful for? What do you see as the other treasures in your life?

Relationships with those we live, work and play with can be greatly enhanced by using the tools we have outlined here. Notice what a difference it makes when you acknowledge others for what you appreciate about them. Use the following ideas to generate remembrances of appreciation for those in your own circle:

To a colleague	"Your ideas in the meeting today were so refreshing...they really helped me break out of an old pattern on that project."
To a housemate	"I love it when you make dinner for us. Thank you for making it feel so festive around here."
To a service person	"It's such a relief to be able to count on you. I really appreciate the quality of work you do."
To a child	"You amaze me. You are wonderfully creative. I love seeing what you'll come up with next!"
To an elderly passerby	"What a great hat. It really makes you look saucy."

Heartfelt acknowledgement like this costs us nothing and yet it can really boost the recipient's day and makes us feel pretty good, too.

Part of the work I do with clients is help them design a lifestyle that feeds and pleases them on every level. Many clients undertaking this kind of transformation have incorporated gratitude rituals into their daily routine. What kind of five-minute ritual might you enjoy creating? What would give you a sense of peace and help you remember the treasures you already hold?

"When Teri suggested I craft a gratitude ritual, my initial reaction was that I was willing and curious to know more, but I wondered about my ability to be consistent. I wasn't prepared for the powerful shift that occurred. I was surprised by the peacefulness that fell over me. It was the weirdest sensation; I relaxed almost to the point of feeling liquid. I don't meditate, but I've read about people feeling like this during meditation. Those moments of pure relaxation as I start my day allow me to be more centered and I've seen more of what I want begin to happen. It is as if the act of expressing gratitude creates an opening up for more to flow easily into my life. That feeling of opening up also takes me into a deep place of just being…like I am liquid flowing into a quiet holding place. Afterward, that feeling stays with me almost at a subconscious level…there is an awareness of it just beneath the surface." — Dani Baker

● ● ●

"Gratitude, like faith, is a muscle. The more you use it, the stronger it grows, and the more power you have to use it on your behalf. If you do not practice gratefulness, its benefaction will go unnoticed, and your capacity to draw on its gifts will be diminished. To be grateful is to find blessings in everything. This is the most powerful attitude to adopt, for there are blessings in everything."
— **Alan Cohen**

When we give for the joy of giving, without expecting something in return, we are expressing gratitude. We are saying to the Universe, "My cup is full to overflowing and I am grateful. This feels so wonderful I want to share it with others." We can express that in many ways: by donating time or resources to a cause we support, by telling those we care about how much they mean to us, or by spending a little extra time with someone who is lonely or in need of extra attention. What if we all let the place where we feel most blessed be the place where we pass it on? Those who feel especially fortunate in their work could be mentors to young people entering the field. People who have warm, comfortable homes could give time or money to Habitat for Humanity. Those who are happy in their romantic relationships could be generous in hosting events where they include single friends that might click. There are many ways to incorporate gratitude into our lives.

For Reflection

1. Which ideas from this chapter resonated with you and how would you like to blend them into your routine?

2. What do you think you might gain?

3. When would you like to begin?

Make Meaningful Contributions

*"When you are inspired by some great purpose,
some extraordinary project, all of your thoughts
break their bonds; your mind transcends
limitations, your consciousness expands in every
direction, and you find yourself in a new, great and
wonderful world. Dormant forces, faculties and
talents become alive, and you discover yourself to be
a greater person by far than you ever dreamed
yourself to be."*

— **Patanjali (1ˢᵗ-3ʳᵈ Century, B.C)**

Your Joy is a Light to the World

The most meaningful contribution we can make is to live a joyful life. By living our own happiness, we become an example—a light that says to others, "it *can* be done."

What is a meaningful contribution? It is your gift to the world. It is something that you value and cherish and want to share with others. It is you saying, with exuberance, "I found so much pleasure in this I want to you to have some, too." It is a genuine feeling of abundance and heartfelt desire to spread that around. Here are a few of the contributions of others that I am enjoying:

- Musicians who share their song and sweep me up in the joy they're feeling. Think Ray Charles, B.B. King,

Nora Jones, Lyle Lovett and Willie Nelson

- Fashion designers and people who dress with a flair that says, "I'm celebrating life today!"

- Writers who share their point of view and in so doing, uplift others

- People who nurture their loved ones by cooking wonderful meals

- People who make their yard a welcome place of beauty and color

- Caregivers who tend the animals with whom we share this planet

- Artists and craftsmen who create objects of beauty that uplift and serve us

- Parents who look for the very best in their children and acknowledge them when they see it

I believe each of us is always contributing to the whole, whether we realize it or not. Some of our contributions are intentional and some are not, but we really can't turn it off. We can, however, choose to make our contributions more deliberate. For example, if I'm feeling sorry for myself and moping and complaining, those thoughts, words, and feelings are travelling out like ripples on a pond and affecting others. When I choose to focus on something more positive, those thoughts, words and actions travel outward as well.

Have you ever been on the highway when there was someone anxious, agitated and in a hurry coming up behind you, zipping in and out of lanes and as they approached you could feel the anger and impatience? So did everyone else. Yet, haven't you also been waiting to turn into a long line of cars and one kind person stopped and waved you in with a smile?

Is it Life Enhancing?

We can contribute to the overall good in every situation, simply by developing the mindset of choosing the thought or action that is life enhancing. Ask, "does this enhance my life or detract from it?"

 My dear friend, Kate, is an amazing example of how we can contribute on many levels. A few years ago, she decided to get a dog, so she went to the local shelter and chose a dog that was older, not terribly cute, not likely to be adapted first. She wanted to give a home to someone who might not have had a chance at one, otherwise. Her dog, Mesa, has given her years of devotion in return.

About once a month, Kate goes to a social service agency and stays overnight with the women who have no place to go. She gives them the most precious gifts we can give another: love, acceptance, time and attention. For the past couple of years, she has also participated in the Susan G. Komen 3-Day Walk and raised thousands of dollars for breast cancer research. This year, she is leading a team, teaching women of all ages and backgrounds how to prepare for a marathon and find joy in the process. For over two decades, she has regularly donated blood and platelets to our local blood bank. Most recently, she bought a hybrid car—not only because it will preserve our natural resources—but also because she wanted to be one of the first buyers so that others would know someone who owned such a car. She was willing to be a guinea pig in order to positively influence the purchase of these more earth-friendly vehicles. Kate is an extraordinary example of living one's values and making conscious choices. Hats off to you, friend.

●   ●   ●

Each of Us Brings Many Gifts

We will give of ourselves in many different situations and settings throughout our lives. Children in our families give us many gifts. Among my favorite are their joyful discoveries and firsts. I felt the same delight my daughter did when she first laid eyes on colorful, saltwater fish. It was such a joy, we returned to the aquarium and many pet stores time after time. There isn't any one right way to contribute to the good of all. In our families, there are those who will contribute to the financial health of the group. Some will keep the home orderly and cook wonderful meals. Some will make beautiful gardens. Some will teach and care for the children. Others will take care of the animals, collect the mail, do the laundry or take out the trash. Each part of the whole is important. Every contribution is a gift from someone.

A large part of the value in each of what we offer is the spirit in which it is offered and accepted. When someone lovingly folds our laundry and puts it way for us, and we receive that gesture with sincere appreciation, everyone benefits. We have a choice with each small act we perform. We can offer it grudgingly or in the spirit of love. We also have a choice in the way we receive from others.

The same principles that work in loving families hold true everywhere else. In governments, companies and organizations of every kind there are myriad tasks to be done for each to thrive. Every job has the potential for spreading light or darkness. We are at choice in each moment, every step of the way, from the moment we are born clear through eternity. We all have the opportunity to offer our best. Some of us will be great listeners who help others clarify their intent. Some will make us laugh, lightening the mood for everyone. Some will be great teachers, some will inspire us and some will challenge us.

We have the power to contribute meaningfully in our chosen work or works. This is one reason why it is so important to choose work that is personally gratifying. In my coaching practice, I often encounter people who believe they are stuck in a career that brings them very little joy or satisfaction. They are strictly continuing for the paycheck. We have much more freedom and power to create lives that satisfy than most of us realize. There are ways to bridge one kind of work to another more suitable endeavor without a major disruption. Here are a few ideas:

- Begin getting experience in a new field by volunteering some of your time there. This puts you in a place of seeing what it is really like and begins your network in that arena.

- Ask for projects that allow you to express the aspects of you that you want to grow.

- Let the new pursuit begin as a hobby and rather than using your free time for things like watching television, begin to hone your abilities through exploring this hobby with classes or hands-on experimentation.

- Start talking with others who are doing what you want to do. They may become role models or mentors that will be of great value to you as a resource and a joy to be around.

- Cultivate friendships with a wide variety of people. They offer fresh and different perspectives that can grow you in ways you haven't thought of.

We are so much more than we think we are. We contribute on a massive scale to all of humanity when we sing, hum, smile or dance. We contribute healing when we forgive. We contribute love and light when we embrace and accept another. We contribute to all creatures when we pray for peace. Remember that we are all jointly creating this experience of life and we are all connected one to another.

> *"How does one become a butterfly?" she asked. "You must want to fly so much that you are willing to give up being a caterpillar."*
> — From *Alice in Wonderland*

 For Reflection

What are the contributions you want to make to each of the following areas in your life?

- Your life journey

- Your life partner

- Your children

- Your extended family

- Your circle of friends

- Your community

- Spirit

- Your creative growth and exploration

- Your work

- Humor in your relationships

Speak Your Truth and Be Willing to Hear Theirs

Honesty is one thing we can each contribute that will benefit the whole, whether it is family, work, school or some other affiliation. Let's be real with each other and allow other people to see who we are. Allow others to experience the authentic you; share your views and ideas when asked. You don't have to convince anybody of anything or defend your position, just be honest about what it is. I see so many trying to pretend to be what they think others want and expect and they lose touch with who they really are. Begin to have honest communication about what you stand for, what is important to you and what your expectations are in each relationship.

Believe In Each Other

As I think about those who have helped me develop as a person, my thoughts turn to those who love me unconditionally, believe in me and expect the best of me. Partly because they hold me in such high esteem, I hold myself that way. When others have confidence in us it lends strength to our conviction of our own capabilities. We don't want to let them down, and that gives us the perseverance to carry on over obstacles that might have stopped us without the vote of confidence from another. One of my greatest teachers was my father, particularly because we disagreed on many issues. He taught me how important it was for me to be true to my own convictions by trying to persuade me to see things his way. Debating with him as a young person was where I learned to articulate my thoughts under fire. Later, I became a member of the high school debate team and today, I love engaging in conversation with a wide range of people holding different views. They are so fascinating, and I've learned that each person's view is as valid as any other; it is just one perspective in the universe, even if it is mine.

Great Learning Comes from those Who Push Our Buttons

If you allow yourself to look back at the real contributions others have made to your growth, especially at the difficult people in your life, you may be amazed. Sometimes our greatest learning comes from those who try us most. They teach us what is most important to us by pushing our buttons. Without those strong responses, we might never know how deeply we feel about certain issues. Who are the ones who push your buttons today? What are they reinforcing in you?

> *"Let a man radically alter his thoughts, and he will*
> *be astonished at the rapid transformation it will*
> *effect in the material conditions of his life."*
> — **James Allen**

We Touch People in Ways We May Never Know

Last summer, my mate and I went out to a drive-in burger restaurant for lunch. It was a beautiful day, middle of the work-week and we were discussing some challenge one of us was navigating. We finished our meal and I turned to fasten my seatbelt.

We were in his pickup truck, so I looked down on the convertible next to us and noticed the top was down and just as I was looking that way, a young man looked up at me and gave me one of the sweetest, friendliest smiles I've ever received. I was touched by it and smiled back. The exchange only lasted a moment, but the energy of that smile lifted me to another place, another vibration. It reminded me of the basic goodness I've always felt in my fellow humans. It put me in touch with the reality that we are all in this together and at our center, we are each an expression of Divinity. I told my mate about the smile, and he was touched, too. The interesting thing about this story is that each time I tell it, tears well up in me and the person or group I'm telling it to, as we all connect back to that moment of joy I felt last summer. This young man likely has no idea of the gift he gave when giving me that smile. We are contributing all the time in ways we do not realize. We cannot help but make our contribution no matter where we are in our lives, or our careers or our spiritual development.

> "Too often, we underestimate the power of a touch, a smile, a kind word, a listening ear, an honest compliment or the smallest act of caring, all of which have the potential to turn a life around."
>
> — Leo Buscaglia

Trust that you are enough and that you are adding value to all that is, in many ways, every moment of every day simply by the thoughts you think. There is no separation between our Creator and us. There is no separation between any of us. Whatever we achieve for ourselves, we make it more available for everyone who wants it. So, with each goal we reach, we give to every person who holds that goal, and they do the same for us. With each insight we gather, the whole moves up a bit. With each joyful moment we experience, we give a lovely gift to all.

Embrace Abundance

We Are Only Limited By Our Thoughts

We live in a universe of amazing abundance. Provided we are willing to see it, the natural world shows us prosperity and abundance in every direction. Raise your awareness to the bountiful diversity in nature: myriad varieties of landscapes, waterscapes, plants, animals, birds, and people, each designed to ensure there will always be plenty.

For example, we have a large maple tree on the hill behind our home; we have nicknamed her Mother Maple, because she has so many offspring. Each fall, her seeds spin all over the yard by the hundreds, looking like little helicopters landing all around us. There will never be a shortage of maple trees here. We go around pulling them up like weeds in the spring, marveling at nature's idea of more than enough.

> *"All the resources you will ever want or need are at your fingertips...There is nothing you cannot be or do or have. You are Blessed Beings; you have come forth into this physical environment to create. There is nothing holding you back, other than your own contradictory thought."*
>
> — Abraham

How are people different when they embrace the idea of an abundant universe? They see no need for war because they no longer hoard, but share their resources. They are not jealous because they know that love multiplies as it is shared. Instead of feeling envy when a friend or colleague reaches a dream, they celebrate, because they know it's possible for all of us to reach our dreams.

They don't express greed because there is no need for greed when the supply is bountiful. They are not hurried or stressed out about time, because they know they have plenty of time for everything that really matters to them. They don't worry about money because they realize that, like everything else, money is energy and it has a natural ebb and flow, just like the ocean. Having a sense of abundance removes fear and gives a sense of peace.

"Man is so made that when anything fires his soul, impossibilities vanish."
— Jean de La Fontaine

You can begin to incorporate this idea of overflowing abundance a little at a time. Here are a few ideas:

- Give yourself an extra 15 minutes to get ready in the morning. Move slowly and notice what you enjoy about your morning routine.

- Be generous in your affection this week with friends, family and pets. Imagine tapping into a resource of unlimited love and allowing it to flow through you to others.

- Build a surplus in one area. For instance, when my husband took on this exercise, he bought a large supply of toilet paper and has maintained that for three years. What a nice thing to never run out of!

- Be extra generous in tipping a service person the next time you go out. Do it with a sense of having plenty and really wanting to share.

- Instead of hoarding those clothes in your closet that no longer fit, make room for new clothes and share with a friend or service agency. You'll make their day and send a message to yourself that there will always be more.

- Begin using abundant language as a matter of course:

  "I have more than enough."

  "There is plenty to share."

  "Please take some tomatoes; we can't possibly eat them all.

- When you find a real bargain for yourself, pick one up for your friend, too. It will make you both feel great.

"My life today looks much different than it did two or three years ago. Back then, I based most of my decisions on a sense of scarcity. No matter how much I made, it seemed like it would never be enough. I was concerned about having enough to pay the bills, to retire, to send my girls to college. There was a lot of fear and worry. Two things happened that really turned things around for me. First, I started working with a coach and looking at the fact that I had a choice: did I want to continue living my life in fear or make a change? I decided to work on my attitude, and with the help of my coach made some major shifts. The other part of that, is when my attitude began to shift, I was willing to look at my spiritual life again, after having given up on that for a long time. I took part in a workshop that opened the door for Spirit to speak to me and become a partner in my life.

"This month, we just celebrated the best year in business we have ever had. I made more money and worked *less*. My idea of abundance incorporates more than money; I want to have an abundance of time, of friends and experiences. I believe there are certain elements that will help anyone who is looking for more abundance in their lives. I see these as having a spiritual direction that supports you, believing in yourself and your ability to truly manifest what you want in life, and surrounding yourself with people who will love and support you in your goals. Also, in the sad times when you are facing big issues, keep a sense of perspective. This is just one more step on your journey. And, I think humor is a must. "Because of the changes I've made, I'm a much happier man today. Life is more fun and I'm aware of how much more is out there for me to enjoy. Nothing can hold me back except me. I believe I've only barely scratched the surface of what I can create and that's pretty exciting. Life is good." – Joel Skillingstead

●   ●   ●

We Are Limitless

What does it mean to you to say you want a life of abundance? Do you imagine a hefty bank balance, plenty of cash and all your bills paid? Ironically, many people think of prosperity in financial terms only, yet this puts a limit on the very idea. Having an abundant life means having enough of everything to share: plenty of time to enjoy your life, make your discoveries and share with those you love. A rich life would also include good health, plenty of energy, ample space for your family, and a limitless supply of ideas and opportunities to pursue.

When we focus on financial prosperity alone, we make the gravest of errors: believing that we must trade most of our life energy in order to have it. What quality of life do we really have when we spend all our time (or a disproportionate amount of it) earning money that we'll be too tired to spend? What about having an abundance of time to explore your passions, your interests and curiosities? How much time would you like to invest in your own spiritual growth and personal development?

We live in a world that encourages us to exchange so very much of our life energy for the pursuit of money and the status it can buy. We say by our actions that it is the most important thing to consider. We trade away the precious childhoods of our offspring for expensive cars, impressive houses and jobs that deplete us until we feel empty. We ask our children, "What are you going to be when you grow up?" and even they understand that we are asking them how they will earn their living. Then we begin to prepare them for it at the tender age of five.

How different our world might be if we spent time learning *who* we are and exploring our curiosities, natural inclinations and capabilities.

 For Reflection

1. How would your thinking change if you believed there would always be plenty of everything you require?

2. How would your choices change if you knew you were infinitely loved by a Divine Creator and everyone else, at their soul level?

3. How do your ideas about scarcity affect your feelings about time? About money? About love and loved ones?

4. What would a shift in thinking about having plenty do for your wellbeing?

Exercise

Finish these statements:

- If I had plenty of time, I would

- If I had plenty of money, I would

- The biggest thing money would give me is

- If I were well loved and acknowledged by friends and family, it would feel

- If I truly could choose to do any kind of work and know I would be successful, I would

- If I had a deep reservoir of physical energy and vitality, I would

Which one of the statements above did you have the most energy around? What small step might you take in the next week to help that idea along?

◆   ◆   ◆

"Synchronistic events occur when you are committed to taking extremely good care of yourself...a Divine force rallies behind you to support your decisions."

— **Cheryl Richardson**

Begin to notice your dominant thoughts around abundance. This can be kind of tricky, because often, when we think we are focused on abundance, we are actually focused on lack. If we attract what we think about, and we think mostly about lack, then this is what we will continue to create. In the following examples, compare the two statements about the same topic.

I wish I had more money.

I love having money to buy the things I want.

I'd like to have more time to work in the garden, but I don't.

I enjoy working in my garden; it truly delights me

In each of these examples, the first sentence had a focus on lack. There were subtle, but important differences in the second statements. They were pure expressions of what is joyful and what is anticipated, with no concentration on what's missing.

To fully come into our abundance, we must acknowledge and embrace all those places where we *already are* abundant. When we feel it down to our toes, we are attracting more of the same by the vibration we offer.

Want more money? Think and talk about what treasures you will bring home when you have it. Want more time? Think and talk about what you will do with that time, how it will make you happy and then feel it as if it were already yours. Want a new relationship? Talk and think about all the fun things you will do with that person. Think about the stories you'll share with them, the favorite places you'll show them and how wonderful it feels to have a kindred spirit for a partner. If you want to keep a new relationship away, talk about how hard it is to meet people and how few good prospects are out there.

We have amazing powers of attraction and can tune in to the abundance of the universe or the lack in the universe by giving either one our energy and attention.

Allow Creativity to Flow

"Ideas come from everywhere."
— **Alfred Hitchcock**

We are amazingly creative. Look around you for a moment, and note all the objects in the room you are in. I'm seeing an Asian lamp painted with pink dogwood branches and jade leaves. The lamp sits on a side table that is a wooden box with a hinged lid on wrought iron legs. There is a colorful paisley rug on the floor. The desk is dark wood, tall, wide and currently, the drop-down lid is closed so my paper mess is hidden from view. There are other lamps and paintings and decorative elements. Each of those things was an idea in someone's mind before it was born. Picture the major, life-changing technologies that were designed in the last century alone: radio, television, satellites, computers, cell phones, microwaves, air conditioning and the Internet, to name a few. We are surrounded by the products of our collective creativity.

Now, think for a moment about all that you have created in your own life. When you look at your home, family, other relationships, opportunities and experiences, do you realize that you brought it all into your life? When I say that we are creative, I mean *all* of us, not just those earning their living as artists, writers, musicians or those who have created high profile gadgets and technology. I believe all of us truly are creative by nature and have the capacity to invent and design way beyond what we think we are capable of. When I teach art classes to college students, there are always some who hang behind after the first class to tell me how they are not creative or artistic at all, but they love art, so they are taking the class. It happens every quarter.

"I really can't draw a straight line, but I thought maybe a class like this would help me," they'll say. The unspoken message is an advance apology: "Don't expect too much of me, because I'm really not very good." We are often taught that people are either born artistic or not. I don't buy that. The ability to draw, paint, sculpt or play an instrument is a skill that can be learned by anyone who puts time and effort into it. Certainly some will find it easier and more natural than others will, just as some find driving or playing basketball easier than others do.

> *"I've never met a person who couldn't paint, but I've met a lot of people who say they can't."*
> — **Frank Clark, PBS Program, Simply Painting**

We are made in the image of a Divine Creator. We are born to use these amazing powers of observation, intelligence and curiosity to go beyond what has been done before and allow our desires to summon energy through us to create. When we stifle that part of ourselves or shrink away from it for fear of failure, we cut off a major portion of our flow of Source energy. Have you ever noticed how exciting it is when you begin a project that you are undertaking for the sheer pleasure of it? I first noticed it when I began taking art classes and painting in college. I would go for hours and not tire, not get hungry or even stop for a trip to the bathroom until the urgency was great.

> *"It is not how much we have, but how much we enjoy that makes happiness."*
> — **Charles Haddon Spurgeon**

Allowing creativity to flow through us is paramount to allowing joy to flow through us, and yet sometimes we approach the challenges in our lives in the same old way we always have. Often, when working with clients who want to experience more joy, we look at the places that currently are more of an energy drain than a gain. Then, we explore ideas about how to shift that. What happens is that almost everyone is surprised by their ability to get creative in their solutions.

"Make visible what, without you, might perhaps never have been seen."

— **Robert Bresson**

Exercise

Take a look at the following areas and ask which are the ones that would benefit from a fresh perspective or shift of some kind.

- Health and body

- Mental/Emotional state

- Career

- Home environment

- Romantic partnership

- Family relationships

- Friendships

- Spiritual practice

- Financial picture

- Service to others

- Fun and relaxation

After you have chosen one or two to think about for this exercise, ask yourself what you really want in these areas, assuming that anything is possible. Now, mentally invite your creative mind to play with these ideas and come up with some possibilities over the next few days. No need to force an answer. Some creative ideas will bubble up from your subconscious with no effort on your part. See what emerges, and record the ideas in your journal.

◆   ◆   ◆

*"It's like driving your car at night. You never see
further than your headlights, but you can make the
whole trip that way."*

— **E.L. Doctorow**

We can be creative and inventive in all areas of our lives if we choose to. The very people who look at the artwork in our home and say, "I could never do anything creative, I just don't think like that," are the same ones who will wow me with their cooking or vacation ideas or beautiful garden. Learn to look at the places where your creativity shows up. Perhaps you have an ability to put order into chaos and people ooh and ahh over your closet organization. Maybe you can look at a trellis at the garden store, then recreate it in your garage two hours later. You could be a parent of four children who has found a way to spend time with all of them and help each feel like they are your favorite.

 For Reflection

1. What would give you joy simply in the pursuing and learning about it?

2. Where is your curiosity naturally drawn now?

3. When might you carve out an hour to explore some creative possibilities for yourself?

4. If you were to challenge your normal way of solving problems and get really creative about that process, what might you do differently to make it fun?

5. What creative pursuits drew you as a child but were put on the back burner when adult responsibilities crowded in? What would it be like to try them again to see if there is still interest?

Spend some time thinking about how you would like to let your creativity flow. As children, many of us were scolded if our eyes and attention wandered to the view through the class window when we were supposed to be working. Today, we are adults and in charge of the way we use our time. Daydreaming is one way to develop creative thinking skills and I wholeheartedly recommend it for about 15 minutes a day. Pick a topic and allow your mind to wander through all sorts of possibilities. Your thoughts may often try to go back to some responsibility held as important; when they do, gently guide them back into the realm of mental play and see what ideas you come up with.

This is not an irresponsible use of time; creative thinking skills serve us well in every facet of our personal and professional lives, *and they are fun.*

 I recently invited a group of colleagues, clients and friends over to create hand-designed greeting cards. One colleague said, "I'm not an artist, Teri, but I will give it a try." I provided paints, brushes and artists materials and they brought blank cards. This colleague had bought beautiful translucent papers with golden leaves printed on them. She began making collages with the papers she'd brought and left with three beautifully designed cards to give to people who are special to her. She was creative even in her approach. She knew her drawing and painting skills might be frustrating, so she chose elements of design that worked well together without having to draw or paint. All she required was the

card, envelope, glue, pretty paper, a cutting instrument and the freedom to allow her creative imagination out to play.

• • •

"If a plant cannot live according to it's nature, it dies; and so a man"

— Henry David Thoreau

Some of you may be in jobs where creativity isn't necessarily encouraged. Perhaps it has been a long time since you simply toyed with an idea to see where it might lead for the fun of it. A few of you might have boundaries and boxes around the kinds of projects that are "appropriate" to your gender. Why limit yourself to what someone else has deemed appropriate? I challenge you to pick a few of the following projects that pique your interest and follow your creative muse wherever it leads. Have fun and be playful about it. These are designed to open the doors of your imagination just a little wider.

Exercise   For Creative Exploration and Play

- Buy a roll of black and white film, load your camera and spend a day looking for subjects that please you. When photography is in black and white, design elements become more prominent. Look for unity and variety, texture and a range of values (intensity from dark to light). By putting your primary object of interest away from dead center, you will create a more interesting composition. See what draws your eye when looking through the lens of a camera.

- Imagine that you are a product designer some time in the future and you have been asked to come up with some preliminary ideas and sketches for a personal hover craft. It would be sort of like an automobile that flies. What features would you want in a vehicle like that? How would it be shaped? How would it be powered? How fast would it go? Have fun imagining what it would be like to fly to the grocery store…how much space would you need for storage?

- Choose a room in your home to plan a makeover for. Nothing is sacred, you can alter anything about that room you choose to, from floor to walls to ceiling. What colors would you choose? What functional changes might you like to make? Perhaps you want to make over a bathroom. How could it serve you better? Maybe you'd like to have hooks rather than towel racks, so that it is easy to drape a towel without having to fold it. Perhaps some wall-mounted candle sconces would add to the relaxation ambience. Visit some home design centers for inspiration. Look at interior design magazines. Then, use those ideas as a springboard for your own. Whether or not you go through with the actual makeover, you'll have a great time coming up with ideas and they may spur you to make some real changes.

- Gather some magazines and photos, scissors, glue and a poster board for a collage of the dreams you want to realize. Visualization is a proven method for athletes to improve their game by using their mental powers. You can use the same power to bring whatever you want into your life. Maybe you want a new home, a boat, or a cabin on the water. You might be looking for certain qualities of life, like more fun and friendship or relaxation. As you go through magazines and photos, gather any picture that you feel drawn to without stopping to analyze why. Then as you begin to glue them down, allow your intuition to guide you. You will likely make some discoveries about dreams you are holding that you might have forgotten you have. In any case, enjoy.

◆   ◆   ◆

Assume that you are as creative as anyone else. Look for where your imagination emerges and enjoy exploring and expanding from there. Remember that every element of life can be enhanced by your creativity, from the way you dress to the dinner parties you give, to the solutions you come up with in your parenting or your chosen work. Life is supposed to be fun. Look at a single sunset, and notice the color and grandeur of it. Every day is a blank canvas when you allow your creative spirit out to play.

Foster Friendships

In the closing scene of the movie, *Fried Green Tomatoes*, Jessica Tandy says, "I've finally found out what the most important thing in life is." Kathy Bates looks intently at her older friend and says, "What?"

With a sparkle in her eye and a conspiratorial smile, Jessica answers, "Friends. Best friends."

Remember how easy it was to strike up a friendship when we were children in school? We might have become friends with someone simply because they wore the same red tennis shoes we did. Anything could bring us together. As adults, finding friends isn't as automatic or as easy as it was when we had a built-in social network. Yet, the benefits are just as important to our sense of joy and wellbeing now as they were then; perhaps even more so, as we spend such a disproportionate amount of time working or being otherwise *responsible*.

There are so many ways that friends enhance our lives and all it costs us is a bit of time and planning. I laugh more when I'm with good friends than any other time. Somehow, things that feel so big and bad when I grapple with them on my own are reduced to a manageable size when I see that everyone is challenged with something. When we share our stories with each other, they somehow feel lighter and often someone shares a different perspective that helps me reframe the situation in a more positive direction.

"The ornament of a house is the friends who frequent it."

— **Ralph Waldo Emerson**

One of the things I enjoy most about friends is that they won't let us get too serious or dramatic. There is a twinkle in the eyes and a little good-natured teasing that keeps any of us from wallowing too deep in self-pity. Sometimes they just take the drama and run with it and then we all have a good laugh at the exaggeration.

Other ways friends add value to our lives:

- They love us, support us and believe in our dreams. Encouragement from someone who we know cares about us deeply can mean the difference between going forward to claim a dream or quitting. They lend us courage when our own is hard to find.

- We can share all kinds of events together: cooking, camping, concerts, fundraisers, kids' soccer games, building a deck, pulling an engine...you name it and good pals somewhere have enjoyed it together.

- They are honest with us. They'll tell us if we look like a house in that tight skirt or if the rug we're thinking about really isn't an improvement over that shiny bald head. They'll also let us know (gently) when we are being brats.

- When our friends come from many different sources like work, church, our childrens' sport teams or our own, they bring a variety of experience and knowledge that we may not have been exposed to. We can learn a lot from each other. Everyone has mastery in certain areas and friends are willing to share that.

- We can be a resource to each other, introducing new people that may turn out to be spouses, business alliances, service providers, clients or just good buddies.

- They can bring fresh perspectives to every area of life. Each of us has a lifetime of experiences and observations to draw from and we can sometimes get into ruts in the way we think. A friend's perspective can shed new light on a situation and be of tremendous value in helping us. We can be pretty tough on ourselves and a friend can show us another side of the story…one in which we have made more of a positive impact than we might know.

- Good friends help us celebrate the achievements and milestones in life and add sweetness to the celebration. When you are genuinely happy for someone else's accomplishment, doesn't it feel great?

- Having a workout buddy is extremely beneficial in staying with a fitness program. We hold each other accountable and inspire each other to keep going even when we're feeling lazy.

- Friends can be such a comfort when we grieve. They can hold us or simply stand quietly in our presence and lend their strength.

- In the best and worst of life's moments we are blessed by friends who share a spiritual base and meditate or pray with us.

- Taking a class with a friend doubles the pleasure. Learning together is a joy even when the class or teacher turns out to be a dud, because we can always laugh at it together.

- Animal friends add an immeasurable sense of comfort, companionship, play and a sense of home to our lives. We have three cats that make me feel so loved and add laughter to every day.

"Help others get ahead. You will always stand taller with someone else on your shoulders."
— **Bob Moawad**

About fifteen years ago, my best girlfriend and I decided that nurturing our friendship and enjoying each other was the priority and we agreed not to let little things get in the way of that. For instance, we agreed that if one of us forgets to give the other a birthday gift, we will not get angry because that's not the important part of our friendship. As the years have gone by, there have been a few times when one of us forgot a special occasion and it was such a relief not to have the other be upset. Now, we occasionally buy an extra of whatever we think the other would like and send it "just because."

Talking frankly about what the expectations and boundaries are in a friendship is important. If one person likes to drop by and the other likes to be called first, some kind of compromise is called for. Many friendships die because one person steps on another person's toes and then gets the cold shoulder, never knowing exactly why they've been dropped. If a friend is important to you and you get the cold shoulder, ask them to be honest with you. By the same token, don't be afraid to say, "Hey, friend, you're stepping on my toes there. Would you go a little easier on that topic?" We are so afraid of confrontation or making someone uncomfortable, that many of us quietly seethe inside instead of asking directly for what we want. How else is the other person supposed to know?

> *"You can make more friends in two months by becoming interested in other people than you can in two years by trying to get other people interested in you."*
>
> — **Dale Carnegie**

Exercise

Are you willing to see where you stand on the friendship scorecard? Take a look at the following statements and rate your skill on a 1 to 10 scale, 10 being the outstanding best.

_____ I make friendship a priority and invest in these relationships on an ongoing basis.

_____ I keep the commitments I make to friends to the best of my ability.

_____ I am flexible to change plans and don't get angry when someone needs to reschedule.

_____ I am supportive of friends and glad when they achieve things that bring them happiness.

_____ I am a good listener and hear what is being said without merely waiting for my chance to jump in.

_____ I am willing to try new things with friends: restaurants, events, music, including new people, etc.

_____ I respect my friends' privacy and boundaries. I don't pry or try to get them to break their own agreements.

_____ I don't always have to have my own way. I'm willing for others to have a chance to choose the movie we see, the restaurant we dine in, the music we listen to, etc.

_____ I don't hoard my friends. I'm willing to introduce people who I think will enjoy each other.

_____ I'm not a user. I try to keep the exchange between us even. We alternate hosting dinners, driving, coming up with ideas and initiating contact.

_____ I am honest in my communication with friends. I don't make up excuses to get out of things. I tell the truth even if it is, "I really just want to stay home and read tonight."

_____ I am generous with friends without being a scorekeeper. I trust them and give them a wide margin for error.

_____ I am honest with myself and when I have no interest in fostering or continuing a friendship, I let it go.

Where would you like to make changes in your friendship skills? What are one or two things you would be willing to work on in the next few weeks?

♦   ♦   ♦

"Friends and family are what make life worthwhile. I am very blessed, I have six or seven very close friends that I let my hair down with, cry with, tell my secrets, fears and dreams to. My friendships nurture me by helping me grow. They let me know that I am loved, needed and wanted. My best friends are people with integrity and honesty. We have some of the same interests and I can talk to them about anything. They trust me as I trust them, listen to me as I do them, know that if I happen to do something that hurts them that it is not intentional but will tell me what I have done that was hurtful, will accept my forgiveness as I would accept theirs. They like to spend time with me and vice versa." — Diane

● ● ●

Awareness and Action

How satisfied are you with:

- The number of friends you have?

- The quality of friendships you are currently in?

- What would you like to change?

- How much time would you like to be spending with friends each week or month?

- What are some steps you could take to bring that about?

- In one or two paragraphs, describe what success in this area would look like to you, being very specific, even as to how you would feel:

Review this often and visualize the picture you describe. Then, let the action you take be *inspired* by the vision you hold.

For Reflection

Ten Ideas for Fostering New Friendships

1. Join a book club, or form one and meet once a month. In addition to meeting new folks, you'll probably expand your viewpoint by reading books that you might not otherwise pick up.

2. Host a come-and-go dessert and coffee for your neighborhood, allowing people to drop by between two and four on a Sunday afternoon.

3. Volunteer for an organization in your community that you would like to support.

4. Visit a church or spiritual group and keep trying new ones until one feels right.

5. Invite a colleague or coworker to coffee, just because you would like to get to know them better.

6. Take a class to learn or improve a skill just for fun. Almost everyone likes to take pictures of their family and a photography class would let you improve those skills and spend an hour a week getting to know a whole new group of people.

7. Teach a class on a subject you have mastery in. Most community colleges are open to ideas for new classes on everything from computer literacy to genealogy for their continuing education classes. Let it be something you would enjoy sharing.

8. Join a Toastmaster's club in your area to meet new friends and improve your speaking skills at the same time.

9. Find a walking buddy. Send an email around to your colleagues or acquaintances and ask if anyone else would like to walk together one day a week. You might get more than one taker; you can get to know each other better and improve your fitness at the same time.

10. Sign up for tennis, volleyball or another sport at your local gym, fitness club or community center.

Let your creativity out to play here, and come up with two or three of your own ideas for finding new friends or breathing life into a friendship that you'd like to reactivate.

1.

2.

3.

When we were in our early thirties, my best friend decided to make a drastic career move. She went from corporate human resources to being a cross-country truck driver. That's right, she learned to drive an eighteen wheeler—and she thinks she's not courageous! I knew she'd be training out of state and then be on the road for several years. That was going to leave an awful gap in my life that might be hard to fill. I was used to having the pleasure of her company anytime, as she lived 20 minutes away. I put out a call to the universe, asking for another friend with those same qualities I love about her: great sense of humor, smart, irreverent in the right measure, kindhearted and fun. Within a few days, I met a new acquaintance through my membership in the local Chamber of Commerce. We volunteered to help with the same event, and it was like we'd known each other for years. We laughed until we hurt. It wasn't until some months later that I learned how literally the universe answered my request. She and my best friend not only shared many wonderful qualities, they shared the exact same birthday, down to the *year*. Charlavan and Phyllis, I love you!

●　　　●　　　●

"Our friends will help us if we let them know how. Often, all we need is a little welcome company."

— from ***Walking in This World, The Practical Art of Creativity*** by Julia Cameron

From a spiritual perspective, there is no greater contribution to the world than to be a good friend first to ourselves and then to others. We may have made agreements before we ever were born that this person or that person would be a learning partner and friend in this life experience. Age difference doesn't matter. Neither does gender, race or location. Several years ago, my then nineteen-year-old daughter studied jewelry design with a man in his seventies. Much to her surprise, he became one of her dearest friends. Even though he moved to Colorado at about the same time we moved to Washington, they are still friends and have long phone conversations every couple of months just to stay in touch. In fact, he's become a friend of the whole family. Allow your inner guidance to help you choose and nurture the friendships that will bring the most aliveness and joy. Be willing to let them come from unexpected places, and when they do, treasure them.

Above all, treat yourself like a dear, treasured friend. After all, you are the only one who will be along for the entire journey.

Cultivate the Spirit of Generosity

Feeling Generous Comes from Knowing You Have Plenty

I first learned about the power of generosity as a young professional, when groups from the office would go out to lunch and divide the bill. I noticed that when I gave just enough to cover my part of the bill, it didn't feel nearly as good as when I gave more than my share. The difference might only be a dollar or two. Where else could I get such a good feeling for two dollars? It became apparent that "to err on the side of generosity" was a good way to live my life because it made me feel an abundance of good things.

This spirit of generosity seems to be a key element for most of us in living more satisfying, lighthearted lives. I've been leading workshops on abundance and prosperity and working with clients in these areas for a few years now, and I've noticed that we are quite willing to be generous in the places where we don't feel a sense of scarcity ourselves. If we are feeling lack in a particular area of life, then that is usually a place where old beliefs are driving our thoughts and behavior. This is a great place for growth and healing to occur. If there is anyplace in your life where you hold on tight to something, that's probably a place where a scarcity belief resides.

Here's an example: I worked with a client who is a mortgage broker and making in the $200,000 a year range, yet she was working 80-hour weeks. She came to me because she wanted more balance in her life. When we started to look at why she was working so much, we found that when interest rates were good, she did it because those opportunities were rare and she thought she'd better take advantage of them. When interest rates weren't so good, she thought she had to drive more business to the door. Under it all, we finally uncovered a bag-lady belief. No matter how much money she made, she allowed the fear of becoming a bag lady to drive her hard until she realized how unfounded that belief was.

The thing is, most of us have places where we feel vulnerable to that sense of scarcity: it may show up as being selfish with our time, our love, our money, giving compliments, forgiveness or any number of other places. The best antidote I've found is cultivating our own sense of generosity.

There are three distinct areas where people can focus on in the beginning and doing so can make a huge impact on the quality of their lives and the lives of those they are closest to.

Be Kind To You

It starts with being generous with ourselves. *Every relationship we will have in life is a reflection of the relationship we have with ourselves.* So, how do you be generous with yourself?

- By giving yourself positive feedback. It's a simple shift from your internal dialog saying, "What a putz, why'd you do it that way?" to saying "Hey, not bad for your first attempt. Let's see what happens when you do it again."

- By setting a comfortable pace for yourself. Life is not track event. You get to decide the pace that you thrive in. Be generous with white spaces in your calendar or planner. Give yourself plenty of breathing room between events.

- Allow yourself room for mistakes which are an inevitable part of growth and exploration.

- Honor your preferences. Be generous in allowing yourself to have what you want.

- Trust yourself to do the best you can with what you have on any given day.

- Invest generously in your own wellbeing. Take time to do the things that gave you pleasure when you were a child: lay on the grass and watch the cloud shapes or curl up with an adventure story and your favorite fuzzy blanket.

When working with clients, I recommend they incorporate these changes slowly, one at a time. So, for instance, you could start with being more generous with yourself for a month…notice how it makes you feel, then in the next month move to another area.

 A few years ago my inlaws were visiting and when my mother-in-law got to our kitchen, she exclaimed with delight at the new colorful dishes, towels, and accessories. She got quiet for a moment and I asked her if anything was wrong. She told me that she'd had the same dishes and accessories for years, and it simply never occurred to her to replace any of it unless something broke or wore out. She had never thought of bringing in new color just for the pleasure it would bring her. We talked about how her parents had grown up during the depression era when money was pretty tight and people had to live frugally, and how that wasn't the case for her and her husband. They had plenty, but they were still running old tapes about conserving. She decided that day to go shopping for some new kitchen-ware. It was so uplifting to see her in the stores, delighting in all the new textures, colors and styles to choose from.

● ● ●

Nurture Your Relationships

The next place to expand that sense of generosity is with others. This can have a very positive effect on the relationships you hold dear. You can do that by:

- Giving them a wide margin for error. Let your natural assumption be that they meant well, and choose not to react.

- Allow them to be who they are naturally without criticizing or trying to change them.

- Listen to them with your full attention.

- Love them unconditionally.

- Forgive them when they mess up, whether they have the courage to ask for forgiveness or not. You can still choose to have the courage to forgive.

- Don't be a scorekeeper. I've already mentioned that my best friend and I made this agreement about 15 years ago: we don't keep score on who called whom last or who gave a gift that wasn't reciprocated. We decided that those were minute details, and the real thing important to us is continuing to enjoy our close friendship.

- Be generous in allowing the other to choose what's best for them; if you have plans with someone and they decide to cancel on the day of the event, let that be okay. This takes the pressure off and they will be grateful to you for being able to be honest. Know that there will always be plenty of fun to share.

In my work as a coach, I hear from many people how important it is and how good it feels to have someone *really* listen to them. Several have said they simply don't get that from anyone in their lives. This is such a simple gift we can give to each other. Try it with someone you care about and see what a difference it makes. Listen with your heart, without interrupting and without trying to offer any advice. Just allow that person to be heard.

Trust the Generosity of Spirit

The third area for fostering the Spirit of Generosity is with what I call the Divine Creative Force. Whether you call it God or the Universe or All-that-Is, there is a guiding intelligence supporting us all through the perfection of the earth and her relationship to the sun and other elements in the solar system. The same force that holds the heavens together is there to assist us in holding ourselves together, too.

A generous spirit would see that force as bigger than any one philosophy—big enough to encompass them all. A generous view is one where we would see that in our quest to understand the nature of this Divine Force, we may have made assumptions that were off the mark. We may have projected our own jealousy, anger and vindictiveness outward to a twisted perception of God.

Einstein once said that one of the most important questions we can ask is whether or not the Universe is a friendly place. What is your view of it? What would a truly benevolent and generous creator be like? I believe a generous creator would give us infinite support and love. A generous creator would endow us with all we require to thrive and be happy. A generous creator would have such faith in us that we would be given complete free will to choose whatever we want to create for ourselves. A generous creator would provide an environment that was pleasing to us, comfortable, filled with beauty and all we need to have delicious physical lives.

Once we let go of old misguided beliefs that are based in fear and scarcity, we can embrace a sense of real trust that all is well. We can draw all we need from what we have been provided, and we can see that there is more than enough of everything…enough to share generously. Then, we can live life in the fullness, abundance and joy that is our birthright.

Make Laughter and Play Part of Every Day

Take Yourself Lightly

Sometimes I catch myself and others trying too hard to get it all in and get it all right. We want to be the best we can in all the roles we play. We try to be thoughtful, romantic and supportive of our mates. We put every effort into giving our children all they require to thrive. Our careers often take up the lion's share of our time and energy. Still, we have siblings, parents, grandparents, friends and others we love and want to honor. Shifting into stress is quite easy with all we expect of ourselves. The best antidote I know of in relieving stress and not taking ourselves so seriously is laughter. How long has it been since you enjoyed a good belly laugh that left you breathless?

Laughter and play are core ingredients for a joy-filled life. They are an essential part of the recipe for wellbeing. Have you ever noticed how often in movies there will be a heavy emotional scene where the audience is perfectly still and quiet? Then, that scene is followed by a funny line or two, which breaks the tension. Everyone feels the relief that laughter brings. It feels so satisfying when a story elicits many emotions and laughter is sprinkled in freely. *Life* feels more satisfying when we have a full range of emotions, too. It is part of what lets us know we are alive. Is there enough play and laughter in your days to give you that feeling of contentment?

We've probably all seen the recent reports from medical research on the emotional and physical benefits of laughter: boosting immune function, enhancing respiration and lowering levels of stress hormones[1], to name a few. Laughter feels good, helps us see things from a less serious perspective and leaves us with a sense of happiness that lasts long after.

Watch Animals at Play

When we look at animals, play is a part of their every day. Whales and dolphins leap out of the water for the sheer joy of it. Cats and dogs love playing with all kinds of toys and will often try to tempt their human caregivers into a game of chase or fetch. Watching creatures engage in play is a delightful activity. We recently had a few days of snow here in Washington State. As I looked out the kitchen door, I saw birds frolicking in the huge twirling flakes that were falling. They dipped and swirled and flew back to a tree, where they landed and some of their friends took off and did similar maneuvers. They were taking turns playing in the snow and it was almost like I could hear them saying, "That was cool, but watch me! Did you see that?"

We watched a documentary on wolves recently that showed they have a particular posture that sends the message, "let's play." They jump around and stop, lowering the front of their bodies by putting their forepaws on the ground and leaving their back legs upright. They had a tuft of fur that they used like we would use a ball to play keep-away. The energy and joy they were experiencing was tangible.

We have three cats in our home and they, too take on postures of play in order to get us to engage in a game of chase with them. They will get what we call "bottle brush tail," and run at us from behind a corner, put four paws on us in a jump and then take off like mad, expecting us to give chase. Since I often work from home, those are my favorite breaks during the workday. I'll finish up a client call and be headed into the kitchen for a glass of water when I get ambushed by a cat. I love turning around and chasing them up the stairs. I giggle all the way and feel like I'm eight again. After three or four minutes, we fall on the floor to catch our breaths and they'll come and rub against my arm, purring, as if to say, "that was fun, Teri, thanks for playing with me."

---

[1] Joel Goodman, The Humor Project

Like the animals, we can build play and laughter into our daily routines. Here are a few ideas to get you started:

- Visit a toy store and let the eight-year-old child in you have a treat that invites playfulness.

- Check out a funny video to watch with friends or family. A few of my favorites: *Toy Story, Finding Nemo, Young Frankenstein* and *Nine to Five*.

- Get a regular dose of laughter once a week with America's Funniest Videos on television. They aren't all winners, but there are always three or four that make me laugh aloud.

- Get together with people who like to laugh and play games that bring out your silliness. Share a potluck meal beforehand so that it's easy on everyone.

- Collect fun props that give the urge to giggle. Wear a feather boa to dinner at your grandmother's house…chances are she'll steal it away from you before the evening is over.

- Play with your pets the way you did as a kid.

- Play basketball or catch with your children or the children of your friends or neighbors.

- Look for writers that amuse you. My husband loves to read anything by Dave Barry. I laugh more when I read about the adventures of Calvin and Hobbs by Bill Waterson.

 My good friend and colleague, Mary McCullough uses play as part of her healing technique as a family therapist working with youngsters. "Play offers children and adults an easier way to solve problems; it allows them to access the creative

part of their brain and use intuition to get to what is really going on for them. They bypass the logical, linear way of thinking and resolve issues almost effortlessly by playing their way through emotions that might be scary if approached head on. They are pleasantly distracted enough to act out the challenge and solution using something as simple as a sand tray and plastic animals. There are many delightful ways to arrive at solutions: one particularly satisfying activity is putting together a collage of what you want. I believe we deserve to have play in every day. I personally like to sing and dance. I go to a dance class every week, and I really get into singing along with bands like the Bee Gees in the house, in the car, wherever I am. There is an element of play in almost everything I do, because it makes me happy." Mary is a delight to work with and also hosts an Outrageous Hat party every spring. Playfulness is truly part of who she is.

•   •   •

Halfway through writing this chapter, my family and I took a midwinter vacation in Cabo San Lucas, Mexico. Devoting a whole week to simply having fun was such a joy. We were mesmerized by the sheer beauty of the creamy white beaches and turquoise water. We were stimulated and excited by all the different sights, the sound of the language and lively music. Yet, each of us noticed that it took a full couple of days to completely unwind and relax into the idea of no responsibilities, just play and relaxation. That surprised me, because I think of myself as pretty easygoing and flexible in my day-to-day activities. I lead a fairly stress-free life. If it took me two days to let go and be really mellow, how long might it take someone who is *really* uptight and scheduled to the max every day? How can we reach that place of carefreeness and delightfully fluid grace on a more regular basis? What was so different about vacation that we were able to completely let go of all our issues and just relax? I believe it was the intention that we held. We went for the sole (or soul) purpose of pleasure. The idea was to see new things, feel free of responsibilities, explore, meander or simply sit on the beach and stare at the water. We gave ourselves permission to decide *in the moment* what we wanted to do. There was no other agenda than feeling good and enjoying ourselves. We slept when we were tired, ate when we wanted to, and allowed our curiosity to lead us wherever we wanted to go. How often does that happen in your life? How could you incorporate that kind of freedom and play into a routine that includes work and responsibility? What might it be like to set aside a day or half day a week to indulge in a mini vacation where the only objective is to relax and have fun? What other ways might you incorporate small breaks for yourself and your loved ones to enjoy during the day? Even ten to twenty minutes of pure pleasure with no other concern than to have fun would be refreshing.

 For Reflection

Complete the following statements:

1. The kind of play that I most enjoy is

2. When I think about playing with friends, what most appeals to me is

3. If I were to take a half day to simply enjoy myself, I would like to

4. Taking time out to laugh and play is really an investment in me, because

5. The last time I remember laughing loud was

6. The comedies I have been meaning to watch are

7. I'm willing to cultivate the playfulness in me because

8. On my (our) next vacation, I'd love to

9. I'd love to find a partner and delve into learning
   _____, just for fun

Look for Opportunities to Create Laughter Breaks

My husband, Russell, has been a great example to me for building fun into every day. Here in Seattle, we listen to a radio station called The Mountain, at 103.7 on the dial. I've always enjoyed their music, but about a year ago, Russ got me hooked on what they call their 5:20 funny. Each weekday at 5:20 p.m., they play a portion of a stand-up comic's routine for 3-5 minutes. I find myself eager to wind up whatever I'm working on around 5:15, so I can enjoy that daily dose of comedy. From that, we have discovered comedians that are gifted at tickling our funny bones. Kathleen Madigan and Eddie Izzard are two of our favorites.

As the following example shows, playfulness and fun are also useful tools for navigating some of our more tricky challenges.

David* was grousing about how boring and time consuming all his meetings were. Granted, they were necessary to employ the much-needed changes his company was making, but so much of what was covered didn't directly apply, that he just wasn't into them. Since he was fairly new to the company, his attendance was expected in order to gain clarity of the overall picture. After listening to him for a few minutes, I came up with a challenge.

He was to mentally shift into the character of Yosemite Sam

when he arrived at work, and visualize himself looking, walking and talking like that little sawed-off, bowlegged grouch we loved when we were kids. As I was describing this, David broke into a grin. "I think I can get into this," he said. "What in tarnation are we doin' in another gol-darn meetin'?!" He was embracing the dialog of the character. He chuckled all the way out to the car. So did I, picturing him waddling down the hall wearing chaps, a messy mustache and that horrid, oversized hat pushed back on his red hair, while toting a couple of six shooters. The game we agreed on shifted both of us into a better frame of mind and turned out to be quite fun for David. When we are in a situation that we can't really change, we can always change our response to it by what we are thinking.

●　　　●　　　●

My husband and I like to take on cartoon personas when we are in a playful mood, or even when we find ourselves getting a little too serious. He does a great Elmer Fudd, and it is impossible for me not to laugh even when he's making a request of me that I normally wouldn't want to hear. We both use the voice of the character from *Rocky Horror Picture Show* who answers the door to the mansion. We love to laugh and getting into the spirit of this kind of play allows the actor in each of us to come out.

Invite Your Inner Drama Queen Out to Play

Often, many of us feel that there is a part of our personality that is being ignored or not having its needs met, yet since we are mature, responsible adults, we stuff it down and never say anything about it. This is the perfect place to employ the element of play. Your inner child wants to throw a tantrum? Go ahead! Let the drama begin. Pick a time and place where you will feel free to be the drama king or queen that would win an Oscar. Exaggerate your case, throw yourself across the bed and wail out all the injustices you're feeling. If you have a friend or partner who is willing to play along, you can even one-up each other and give an award to the saddest sack of all. This is the perfect place to use your acting skills. Stomp your feet, shake your fist and vent your troubles. Before long, you'll be laughing at yourself. More importantly, you'll have a good time and that part of you that hasn't felt like it was being heard will be satisfied and you may discover some useful information in the process.

As parents, we can employ playfulness in diffusing emotionally charged moments with our children. Ask them to voice their issue in the character of their favorite cartoon. It immediately takes the edge off and they are learning valuable coping skills they can use from now on. It's pretty hard to take things too seriously when they say, "my life is over," in the voice of Donald Duck.

Savor the Gifts That Delight You

I believe most of us could be having so much more fun and such a richer, more colorful experience than we are having now, simply by changing our approach just a little. Life isn't meant to be endured. It is meant to be a joyful, amazing adventure. Look at all that was put into place for our enjoyment. Note the variety of delights to our senses: we are serenaded by the sounds of leaves rustling in the wind, birds singing, waves crashing, loved ones laughing and talking, incredible music and many beautiful languages. Our eyes feast on stars sprinkled on a velvety black sky, myriad brilliant flowers, lush fields, majestic mountains, canyons, forests, oceans, still clear lakes, rivers, streams, rock formations, animals, fish, birds and other creatures.

There are so many delicious and tantalizing scents: spices, bread baking, flowers, summer rain, pine forests, a freshly cut lemon or orange and the scent of someone we love are only a few. There is so much in place in this life that is truly a gift to us. There are so many reasons to be joyful and my wish for you is that you begin to embrace them and open yourself to a greater measure of happiness than you ever dreamed possible. Laughter and play come naturally to a heart that is full of joy.

Allow that part of you to be free to express in any way that feels right. This is where our creative impulses come from. Some of us will be so happy that our voices erupt into song when we're soaring. Favorite memories of my father are the sounds of him singing as he shaved, and whistling as he went about his work. His crew gave him the nickname of Happy, and it was fitting. His joy was contagious and your joy will affect others, too. You may be moved to restore an old car. Many will want to dance. Some will be inspired to design a new garden or pick up a camera and capture some beauty. There is no one right way to do anything. Assume that whatever way you express your happiness is perfect for you. Appreciate others when you see them living in the flow and joyful. Use this chapter and this book as a way to tweak the design of your own life so that it pleases you more. This is your map for joy; use it well.

Choosing and Working With a Personal Coach

When I was in my twenties, I longed for someone who could help me be more of what I wanted to be but didn't quite know how to get there. It wasn't until about a decade later that I heard about the personal coaching profession and learned about the requirements for becoming certified in this field. After taking the first class, I recognized the power of having an advocate like that work with people to achieve their dreams, and completed full certification.

The coaching industry has experienced phenomenal growth over the last few years, which means there are more qualified coaches to choose from than ever before. They specialize in many fields, and have sub-specialties that come from other life and business experience. For example, I am primarily a business and executive coach, and I love helping people re-design their lifestyles to allow for more joy and abundance. There are coaches who specialize in relationships, spiritual fulfillment, public speaking, career transitions and dozens of other niches.

Here are several reasons why you might choose to hire a coach:

- You want to change your lifestyle so that it fits the person you *really* want to become.

- You want to improve your performance on or off the job.

- You want to develop in a particular skill area.

- You would like to have support while making a major career or life transition.

- You have your eye on an executive position and want to add polish and identify blind spots.

- You love your small business, but it is not profitable enough to sustain you.

- You want to find your purpose in life and move toward fulfilling that.

- You know some of your limiting beliefs hold you back but you're not sure which ones are responsible or what to do about it.

- You'd like help in developing a spiritual practice and being at peace with that side of yourself.

So many times, we struggle along, wanting to make changes but not sure how to go about it and falling into the same old rut. I believe coaching is a powerful way to partner with someone to help you see what you aren't seeing. You don't have to do it alone.

If you are looking for a coach to work with, here are the guidelines I recommend:

- Know what you want to get from the relationship; be clear about why you are hiring a coach and what success would look like to you.

- Choose someone who has experience and training that satisfies your standards. There are a lot of folks out there calling themselves coaches who have not professionally prepared themselves for that role. Ask how and where they got their training. My first choice would be to work with someone who studied in an organization that was licensed by the International Coach Federation. There are probably some excellent coaches who didn't complete formal studies, and I believe they would be the exception rather than the rule. As in any profession, continued learning and growth is important and the standards of the coaching profession are continually rising. Those who are committed to excellence will demonstrate that by continuing to learn new skills and "sharpening the saw."

- Have a meeting or conversation with a few potential coaches before making your selection. There will likely be one that feels like a better match for you. Personal chemistry is essential in a relationship like this. You want to be comfortable talking with them about the intimate details of your life and thoughts. This requires a high level of trust. If a friend or colleague is working with a coach they like and are getting good results, ask for their contact information and talk to them. If you are working with someone new to you that you've chosen from a web site, ask for references if that brings you more confidence and helps solidify your decision.

- Ask about fees up front. Do enough research to know what the range of fees is in the specialty you are choosing. You will find that information on the profiles of coaches on web sites listed below. Be willing to pay for an experienced coach, if you can afford one. You will see the lowest fees charged by those new to the profession, and while they may be very good, my experience has been that those with a few years under their belts were much more effective in helping me get where I wanted to go.

- See this as an investment in your growth and be willing to commit to doing some important work. This sometimes requires several sessions, since a lot of what holds us back from our success is limiting beliefs that may require some digging to find. You may be asked to look at things no one has ever asked you to examine before. Use the opportunity to further your own development. By the same token, don't be afraid to ask for an alternate exercise or question if the one presented isn't working for you.

- Don't let your geographic location limit your choices. Although some coaches have clients come to their office, the majority offers telephone coaching in addition. That means you can hire a coach anywhere and have your sessions in your pajamas, if you like. Here are a couple of places to look: I've listed coaches I know in a variety of specialties on my web site at www.intrepid-communications.com. You will find more comprehensive lists and profiles at

www.coachu.com

www.comprehensivecoachingu.com

www.coachfederation.org

I wholeheartedly believe in the power of coaching to improve lives. One of the biggest values coaches offer is what we call level-three listening. That means we are listening not only to what you say, but how you say it, and the energy we feel coming through the words. We look for the message behind the words using our intuition. Simply having someone listen to us at that level is very validating. It allows for the client to uncover and articulate deeper understanding of their own beliefs than they might achieve on their own. May your own route to personal development be perfect for you.

Resources

Books

If Life is a Game, These are the Rules, by Cherie Carter-Scott (Broadway Books, 1998)

Celebrate Yourself: Enhancing Your Self Esteem, by Dorothy Corkille Briggs (Doubleday, 1986)

Wishcraft: How to Get What You Really Want, by Barbara Sher (Viking, 1979)

Excuse Me, Your Life is Waiting, by Lynn Grabhorn (Hampton Roads Publishing Company, 1999)

Living Your Best Life, by Laura Berman Fortgang (Jeremy P. Tarcher/Putnam, 2001)

Feel the Fear and Do It Anyway, by Susan Jeffers (Fawcett Books, 1992)

Divine Intuition: Your Guide to Creating a Life You Love, By Lynn A. Robinson, M.Ed., (Dorling Kindersley, 2001)

Small Miracles — Heartwarming Gifts of Extraordinary Coincidences, by Yitta Halberstam and Judith Leventhal (Adams Media Corporation, 1998)

How to Say No Without Feeling Guilty:And Say Yes to More Time, More Joy and What Matters Most to You, by Patti Breitman and Connie Hatch (Doubleday, Broadway, 2000)

Conversations with God, by Neale Donald Walsch (G.P. Putnam, 1996)

Blessing: The Art and the Practice, by David Spangler (Riverhead Books, 2001)

The Artist's Way: A Spiritual Path to Higher Creativity, by Julia Cameron (Jeremy P. Tarcher/ Putnam, 1992)

The Tao of Abundance, by Laurence G. Boldt (Penguin, 1999)

Creating Money: Keys to Abundance by Sanaya Roman and Duane Packer (H.J. Kramer, 1988)

Secrets of Six-Figure Women, by Barbara Stanny (Harper Collins, 2002)

Take Time for Your Life, by Cheryl Richardson (Broadway Books, 1998)

Life Makeovers, by Cheryl Richardson (Broadway Books, 2000)

Creating You and Company, by William Bridges (Perseus Books, 1997)

I Know Just What You Mean: The Power of Friendship in Women's Lives, by Ellen Goodman and Patricia O'Brien (Simon & Schuster, 2000)

Useful Web Sites

www.abraham-hicks.com – Offers uplifting tapes, compact discs, workshops and books all geared toward being a deliberate creator of your life experience.

www.comfortqueen.com – All kinds of ideas for making time for treating you special.

www.hallmark.com – Makes it easy to remember loved ones, friends, and colleagues with e-cards (e-cards are free, and you can also order regular cards and gifts online)

www.bluemountain.com – e-cards for all occasions, no charge.

www.fairytalebrownies.com – These brownies are inexpensive, baked from scratch and sure to make the recipient feel special. You can also order by phone at (800)324-7982.

www.volunteermatch.org – Helps match individuals who want to give to their communities with organizations who need volunteers.

www.massagetherapy.com – Associated Bodywork & Massage Professionals will help you find an appropriate practitioner in your local area and also describes the different kinds of treatments and their benefits.

www.spafinders.com – Helps you find the kind of spa that you are looking for.

Acknowledgments

For inviting me out to play, I thank Spirit. In particular, I thank my long-time guide, Graebel.

For unconditional love and support, I thank my husband, Russ.

For believing in my dreams, I thank my daughter, Andrea.

For asking the question that inspired the idea, I thank Dr. Jeanine Sandstrom and Dr. Lee Smith of Coachworks International.

For her genuine warmth and keen eye, I thank my editor, Marilyn Schwader.

For creative genius, I thank my design and layout partner, Kimberly Skrinde.

For setting the bar high enough to inspire me, I thank Dr. Wells of U.N.T.

For their generosity in participating in this discovery process with me I thank Dani Baker, Joel Skillingstead, Janet McNaughton, Kate Osterfeld, Mary McNaughton and Diane Harter

For the joy they bring to my work every day, I gratefully thank my wonderful clients; your growth, enthusiasm and expanded happiness are the ingredients that hold this book together.

About the Author

Teri Johnson is a business and life coach who helps people re-design their lifestyle so that they are living in homes they love, having satisfying relationships, delightful experiences, and doing work that allows them to shine and thrive on every level. She believes each of us has unlimited potential for growth and happiness and to get there, we must be true to ourselves first and foremost. Teri loves helping clients get clear about what they *really* want and then allowing it to come to them with ease by breaking old thought patterns and self-sabotaging behavior.

Teri has written and published numerous articles and newsletters since 1987, and this is her first book. She is also a public speaker and leads workshops and classes on leadership and coaching within organizations. She currently lives in Washington state, but works with clients from all over the world. She shares her home with her husband of 22 years and three cats. To learn more about Teri and her company, please visit her website at www.intrepid-communications.com